You can do this!

YOU CAN DO THIS

Daily Affirmations to Live Recklessly Alive

SAM EATON

ZONDERVAN®

ZONDERVAN

You Can Do This

Published by Zondervan, 3950 Sparks Drive SE, Suite 101, Grand Rapids, MI 49546, USA. Zondervan is a registered trademark of The Zondervan Corporation, L.L.C., a wholly owned subsidiary of HarperCollins Christian Publishing, Inc.

Requests for information should be addressed to customercare@harpercollins.com.

Zondervan titles may be purchased in bulk for educational, business, fundraising, or sales promotional use. For information, please email SpecialMarkets@Zondervan.com.

ISBN 978-0-310-46742-7
ISBN 978-0-310-46740-3 (audiobook)
ISBN 978-0-310-46743-4 (eBook)

HarperCollins Publishers, Macken House, 39/40 Mayor Street Upper, Dublin 1, D01 C9W8, Ireland (https://www.harpercollins.com)

Art direction: Gabriella Wikidal
Interior design: Kristy Edwards
Photography (back cover): Brittany Todd

Printed in Malaysia

25 26 27 28 29 OFF 10 9 8 7 6 5 4 3 2 1

For my younger self—
and for anyone still daring to dream.
You can do this.

CONTENTS

WEEK 4: THE SPACES THAT SHAPE US

WEEK 5: BREAKING FREE FROM WHAT'S HOLDING YOU BACK

WEEK 6: RECLAIMING YOUR POWER

WEEK 7: CHANGING YOUR STORY

WEEK 8: GROUNDED IN GRATITUDE

WEEK 9: TRUSTING THE PROCESS

WEEK 10: HEARING FROM YOUR FUTURE SELF

WEEK 11: MOMENTS THAT MATTER

WEEK 12: BECOMING WHO YOU'RE MEANT TO BE

WEEK 13: LIVING RECKLESSLY ALIVE

INTRODUCTION

ARE YOU LIVING RECKLESSLY ALIVE?

What does that even mean?

It's not about being fearless or having it all figured out. It's about choosing to show up, even when life feels like a mess, even when you don't have all the answers. It's about living fully, bravely, and on purpose—knowing that even in the hard moments, you are still worthy of joy and meaning.

Is it just for the dreamers, the optimists, the achievers?

No. It's for *you*. I promise. You can live recklessly alive.

Maybe you need a new sense of purpose. Maybe you need a fire inside you again. Maybe you need to feel, for the first time in a long time, that you matter and belong here. Or maybe you need to finally let go of what's been holding you back: weights of the past, old identities, or lies you're tired of hearing.

Whatever it is, wherever you're starting from—you can do this.

You can build the type of future you want to live, one that's rooted in peace, strength, and adventure.

Sounds ambitious, doesn't it? But it's possible. I know because I've been there.

Life wasn't always kind to me. Some days it felt like I was barely holding on, trudging through a fog of exhaustion, hurt, and doubt. I've had my share of dark seasons. I've stumbled and face-planted more times than I can count. Yet here I am, still standing. If you've been feeling stuck, broken, or unsure of how to move forward, hear this clearly: You are not alone.

This book isn't about handing you a magic wand or pretending there's a one-size-fits-all fix for every struggle. But I can share what's worked for me—the raw, real lessons that have taught me how to build a life I never thought possible, one that feels wildly alive, the way it's meant to be.

I invite you to join me on a journey to move forward, day by day, step by step, to inspire you to live a life you want to be living, a life that feels hopeful and full of possibility.

On this journey together, we'll explore seven themes that have been game changers for me and my mental health:

Each day, you'll have a chance to pause, reflect, and anchor yourself with an affirmation. Once a week, I'll offer you a challenge designed to pull you out of your comfort zone to a place where you can start seeing real momentum.

But before we get ahead of ourselves, please know: There's no right way to do this. It's tough to go from a hard standstill to finding your way again. Take it at your own pace. Spend three days reflecting on one entry if you need to. This is your life, your journey. You decide the rules.

I believe in you. I believe in your unpolished, complicated, and beautiful story. And I believe that a life that feels recklessly alive isn't a pipe dream. It's out there, waiting for you.

So let's take this one day at a time. I'll be right here with you.

You can do this.

WEEK 1

EVERYDAY MOMENTUM

GETTING STARTED IS ALWAYS THE HARDEST PART. IT'S EASY TO talk yourself out of trying and let your brain swirl in circles of overwhelm and inaction. I've learned the hard way that life isn't always about taking massive, life-changing leaps—it's about finding the courage to do *something* when you'd rather do nothing at all.

This week, we're focusing on small wins that might seem insignificant at first but can shift the way you see yourself. It could be tackling something you've been avoiding, choosing to rest without guilt, or doing one thing that makes you feel a little more alive.

You don't have to do everything at once, and you don't have to do it alone. Let's take this week to start building momentum together, one small step at a time.

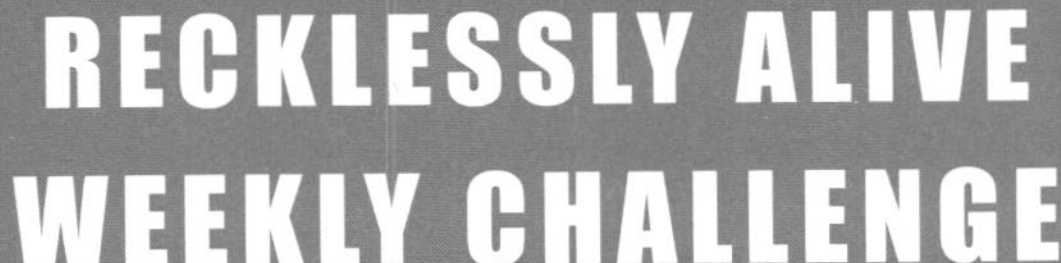

RECKLESSLY ALIVE WEEKLY CHALLENGE

Take one small action each day this week to build momentum in your life. It doesn't need to be complicated or time-consuming; five minutes or less is all it takes. Choose something that brings you joy, helps you feel more alive, or makes the world a little brighter—and take a photo of it. Whether you're reconnecting with a friend, cleaning one drawer, or trying a new recipe, each step counts.

When your brain tells you things will never improve, look back at your daily photos and remind yourself that momentum is building, one small action at a time.

MOMENTUM STARTS HERE

SOME MORNINGS, GETTING OUT OF BED FEELS LIKE SCALING Mount Everest in a blizzard without a coat. The weight of the world presses down, making even the most minor tasks feel impossible. Staying beneath the covers, wrapped in yesterday's exhaustion, can seem like the only way to protect ourselves from the cold, harsh reality outside. When I was growing up, nobody ever warned me how much life can hurt sometimes.

At twenty-three, I found myself in the darkest, most painful months of my life. The voices in my head were relentless, brainwashing me to believe that life would never get better. I wish someone had come into that bedroom, hugged me, and told me this: Your brain can lie to you, and you don't have to believe everything you think.

I've faced many tough moments since—as we all do—but when I'm feeling stuck, one slight shift has always helped me find a way forward. Spoiler alert: It's not winning the lottery, meeting a soulmate, or stumbling across some magic beans that will change you into a supermodel. It's simpler and much more powerful than that.

At these times, I commit to doing one thing every day to improve my life or make the world a better place—one thing every day, especially when I don't feel like it. Willpower alone won't pull you out of a funk. (Aren't we already exhausted enough?) Building momentum begins with one small action. Even the tiniest step forward counts as progress. Even the tiniest step forward is a win.

You don't have to scale a mountain today, my friend. (But if by some strange circumstance you do, you can borrow my coat.) You are stronger than the weight you're carrying, braver than you feel, and more capable than you believe. I know because I've lived it. That butt print in the mud next to yours is mine. So push off those covers—real or metaphorical—and let's ignite your momentum together.

RECKLESSLY ALIVE AFFIRMATION

I CAN DO ONE THING TODAY TO IMPROVE MY LIFE
OR MAKE THE WORLD A BETTER PLACE.

REFLECTION

What's one small action you can take today, taking just five minutes or less, that might help you feel a little more alive, connected, or grounded?

You can do this.

FIGHT AGAINST THE NEGATIVE VOICES

HOW YOU TALK TO YOURSELF CAN SHAPE YOUR DAY. MAYBE YOUR inner voice is kind and steady. Or maybe it's filled with doubt, condemnation, and second-guessing. If the voices in your mind are saying horrible things, like mine did for years, I need you to know that those voices didn't start with you. Somewhere along the way, you absorbed messages, criticisms, and disappointments that were never yours to carry.

When I was twenty-eight, I stared into the bathroom mirror late at night, my reflection blurred by tears and exhaustion. My inner voice attacked me, running through a broken record of every way I didn't measure up and never would. Then, a thought stopped me: *I cannot spend the next fifty years attacking myself.* I looked closer at my puffy, red eyes and realized for the first time that I'd been fighting the wrong battle.

One of the most important aspects of building momentum is fighting back against the negative voices in your head—your self-talk. The way you speak to yourself shapes how you see yourself and the world around you.

Changing that inner dialogue doesn't mean lying to yourself. You can choose a kinder, truer narrative that sounds more like a friend who loves you unconditionally. One tool I've learned is to interrupt my mind when it speaks in absolutes. When I hear, *I'll never be happy*, I counter it with a statement using *yet* or *but*:

- I may not feel happy *yet, but* I can do one thing today that sparks joy.
- I may not be where I want to be, *but* I'm learning and growing every day.

It might feel silly at first, but I encourage you to actually say these statements aloud. Your voice matters, and hearing yourself choose a kinder truth can start to rewire the way you see yourself, even if it feels awkward at first.

Your words are your power to heal, restore, and reclaim your life. Just as those negative voices were learned, they can be unlearned too. Look in the mirror today and commit to speaking words that move you forward. Let your voice be the fuel that propels you toward living fully and recklessly alive.

RECKLESSLY ALIVE AFFIRMATION

I CAN TREAT MYSELF WITH KINDNESS AND SPEAK TO MYSELF IN WAYS THAT STRENGTHEN AND EMPOWER ME.

REFLECTION

Which patterns have shaped the way you talk to yourself? How might your life change if your inner voice shifted from criticism to kindness?

You can do this.

KNOW YOUR WORTH

WHEN A PARENT MEETS THEIR NEWBORN FOR THE FIRST TIME, their face often fills with a love so big it spills over, impossible to contain. The baby hasn't done anything to earn it. They're crying, screaming, and already blowing through diapers like it's a competitive sport. And yet that tiny human is worthy of love simply because they exist. And so are you.

Self-worth is the belief that your value comes from who you are, not what you do. It's the unshakable truth that you deserve love, belonging, and kindness simply because you exist. At its core, self-worth is about knowing that you matter; your existence carries weight and meaning, regardless of the circumstances.

But for so many of us, that belief feels fragile. Life has a way of throwing challenges at us from every angle. Harsh words from others, stinging rejections, and constant comparisons sneak into our minds like unwelcome houseguests. They whisper lies, planting seeds of doubt that grow into feelings of inadequacy. Over time, these messages pile up, slowly chipping away at the foundation of who we are, until we question our worth.

Listen to me, my friend: You don't have to prove your worth to anyone, not even to yourself. You are already enough. So if today feels heavy, if doubt or unkind words are pressing down on you, pause and take a deep breath. Building momentum starts with small shifts: treating yourself with kindness, silencing the inner critic, and choosing to replace those lies with the truth.

Let today be the first step in healing all those negative self-beliefs and moving back toward the truth you carried as a newborn: You are *worthy* of love and belonging. You always have been. You always will be.

RECKLESSLY ALIVE AFFIRMATION

I AM WORTHY AS I AM, AND MY WORTH IS NOT DEFINED BY WHAT I DO OR WHAT OTHERS THINK OF ME.

REFLECTION

Which labels, thoughts, or beliefs have you carried that were never meant for you? What is one truth you can hold on to today about your worth?

You can do this.

FIND THE STRENGTH FROM WITHIN

MY HANDS TREMBLED AS I GRIPPED THE STEERING WHEEL, THE weight of my life pressing down on me. I was drowning in a current of two jobs, graduate school, and endless debt. I sat there, frozen—too overwhelmed to cry, too exhausted to move, and wondering, *How will I ever make it another day?*

That moment felt like rock bottom, but it taught me something invaluable: I am strong enough to crawl forward, even when it feels impossible. And so are you. True strength isn't about being fearless or unbreakable; it's about facing setbacks and finding the courage to rise again.

Despite everything I've been through, I never would have called myself strong or resilient. But that's how most of us struggle. We endure quietly, carrying our battles beneath the surface where no one can see them. We rise each day, not because it's easy but because we have no choice. And in that persistence, when we keep going, we display a strength for which we rarely give ourselves credit.

Building momentum doesn't come from waiting for the perfect moment to act. It's built in those small, unseen decisions to keep trying. It's writing the email your brain says you're not qualified to send, saying yes to an opportunity that scares you, or showing up even when you don't feel like you belong.

So if you're feeling how I was in the car that day, remind yourself, *I'm stronger than I think*. You've already proven it by surviving every challenging moment life has thrown your way. The strength you need isn't something you have to search for—it's already within you. Trust it, lean on it, and keep moving forward. You've got this.

RECKLESSLY ALIVE AFFIRMATION

I AM PROUD OF THE STRENGTH I'VE BUILT AND THE RESILIENCE I SHOW EVERY DAY. I HAVE WHAT IT TAKES TO KEEP MOVING FORWARD.

REFLECTION

What is one moment from your past that proves your strength, even if no one else noticed it? What does resilience look like in your life right now, and how can you remind yourself of it when things feel heavy?

You can do this.

SELF-CARE AS FUEL TO MOVE FORWARD

FOR YEARS, I THOUGHT SELF-CARE MEANT CRASHING ON THE couch, binge-watching TV, or soaking in a bubble bath until I turned into a raisin. And honestly? Some days, that's exactly right. But I've learned that self-care isn't about escaping. It's about coming back to yourself by figuring out what you need to feel steady, grounded, and like *you* again.

Over time, I've found it helpful to think about self-care in six kinds of ways that have made a difference in my life:

- **Physical Self-Care:** Moving your body, getting the rest it needs, and nourishing it, whether that means taking a walk, napping, or simply drinking more water.
- **Emotional Self-Care:** Sitting with your feelings instead of ignoring them. Journaling, crying, or talking to someone you trust can help you process your emotions.
- **Mental Self-Care:** Giving your mind what it needs to feel balanced. This might involve reading, praying, or setting boundaries with technology usage.
- **Social Self-Care:** Connecting with people who lift you up. If you're feeling isolated, the remedy might involve putting yourself out into the world, perhaps joining a community, or reaching out to someone.

- **Spiritual Self-Care:** Finding stillness and meaning in things like meditation, prayer, time in nature, or listening to music.
- **Practical Self-Care:** Tackling tasks that lighten your load, such as organizing your space, meal prepping, or crossing that item off your to-do list.

If you have a million things on your schedule, spending the day in the tub could be the opposite of what you need, so pay attention to what kind of self-care would be most impactful right now. Self-care is the fuel that helps you build momentum. You can't keep moving forward if your tank is running on fumes.

I hope you take a moment today to ask yourself, *What do I need to feel whole, steady, and ready to show up as my best self?* The peaceful, joyful life you're dreaming of isn't some far-off destination. It starts here and now with how you care for yourself—because your needs matter.

RECKLESSLY ALIVE AFFIRMATION

I HONOR MY NEEDS AND CARE FOR MYSELF IN WAYS THAT RESTORE MY ENERGY AND BRING ME BALANCE.

REFLECTION

Which type of self-care do you need most today? How can you take one small step to give yourself that care?

You can do this.

DAY 6

WHEN YOU'VE LOST ALL MOMENTUM

WHEN I WAS A TEENAGER, I FELT LIKE THE WORLD EXPECTED ME to already know my life's purpose. Somewhere, between finding a prom date and fifth-period geometry, I was supposed to have a sky-splitting revelation about what I was meant to do for the next fifty years.

Nobody told me that purpose isn't a singular, fixed destination. It's not a flashing neon sign you stumble upon in a dark forest, spelling out, "Congratulations! You've arrived!" No, our purpose shifts, expands, and takes on new forms with every choice.

While I can't say for sure why we're here on this earth, I believe it has something to do with loving deeply, helping others when they need it, forgiving, healing, and finding the strength to rise again. It's about sitting under the stars, getting lost in enchanting stories, and using our talents to leave the world brighter than we found it. It's showing up as our truest selves, flaws and all, and embracing this wild, imperfect life the best we can with the time we're given.

In the moments when I feel like I've lost all momentum—when the weight of life feels unbearable and it's hard to see a clear way forward—one of the best things I've learned to do is to shift my focus outward. Instead of dwelling on my misery, I try to connect with something bigger than myself.

So if you're feeling lost or weighed down, remember this: Purpose isn't something you have to figure out all at once. It's something you build, moment by moment, in how you show up and how you pour love into the world. When life feels heavy, start small: Help someone in need, create something beautiful, or step outside and let the vastness of the sky remind you how connected we all are.

Your life doesn't have to be perfect to matter. You don't need to have all the answers to make a difference. Keep showing up as you are, flaws and all, and trust that each act of kindness, courage, and authenticity leaves the world a little brighter. That's purpose in motion. That's the beauty of why we're here.

RECKLESSLY ALIVE AFFIRMATION

MY LIFE HAS MEANING, AND MY PURPOSE WILL GROW AND EVOLVE THROUGH EVERY SEASON.

REFLECTION

When you think about the moments that have made your life feel purposeful, what do they have in common, and how can you create more of them?

You can do this.

DON'T GO THROUGH IT ALONE

AT THE END OF OUR LIVES, IT WON'T MATTER WHAT BRANDS OF clothes we wore, what kind of car we drove, or which titles we chased. What *will* matter are the stories people tell about how we made them feel—how we showed up, loved deeply, and let others feel genuinely seen and known.

But love and connection aren't always easy. There's heartbreak when you lose someone you thought would always stay. There's pain when you realize that someone you would have done anything for walked away. Those moments leave scars that feel impossible to heal.

After enough experiences like that, I began building walls. It felt safer to stay guarded than to risk another blow. I convinced myself that isolation was the answer; if I didn't let anyone in, no one could hurt me. But in trying to protect myself, I shut myself off from what makes life worth living.

I've since learned that connection is the heartbeat of a meaningful life. The energy we give and receive from others keeps us moving forward, even when life feels unbearable.

If you're in a season where you feel hurt and alone, I want you to know you're not the only one. I understand firsthand how terrifying it can feel to trust someone with your story, especially when the wounds you're struggling with are fresh. But know this: You are worthy of the community that makes you feel safe, valued, and alive. Just because someone couldn't see your worth doesn't mean no one will.

We were made to be in community. Even when it feels like there's nobody left, there's always a chance to begin again. The right people will see, celebrate, and cherish you. Keep going, my friend. Momentum can start with one connection.

RECKLESSLY ALIVE AFFIRMATION

I AM WORTHY OF DEEP, MEANINGFUL CONNECTIONS.
I OPEN MY HEART TO LOVE, KNOWING I AM NOT ALONE.

REFLECTION

What small step could you take today to open yourself up to connection, even if it feels vulnerable? Who in your life makes you feel safe, valued, and seen? How can you nurture or deepen that relationship?

You can do this.

WEEK 2

COURAGEOUS GROWTH

COURAGEOUS GROWTH IS THE CHOICE TO MOVE FORWARD, EVEN when it's hard. It's saying yes to challenges that scare you, stepping into that discomfort, and trusting that the process of growing will lead you somewhere better. It's not about having all the answers; it's about taking action, facing your fears, and believing in your ability to change.

This week, we're exploring how courageous growth fuels everyday momentum. It helps us chase big dreams, rewrite how we talk to ourselves, and rise stronger after rejection. Growth asks us to show up for the life we want, even when it feels uncertain. Let's take those steps together and see what's possible when courage leads the way.

RECKLESSLY ALIVE WEEKLY CHALLENGE

Write down one goal or dream you've hesitated to pursue because it feels too big or daunting. Commit to taking one actionable step toward your dream this week. Every big, beautiful dream started with a single step—one moment of courage that said, *I'm going to try.* You don't need to have it all figured out. Just begin.

ATTEMPT THE IMPOSSIBLE

DURING MY FIRST CHALLENGE TO TAKE ONE SMALL ACTION EVERY day to make life better, either for myself or for someone else, I signed up for a 5K race. I wasn't a runner. What's the opposite of athletic? But something inside me wanted to prove I could do it. Crossing that first finish line after 3.1 miles, I heard the whisper of something I hadn't heard in a long time: *Maybe I'm stronger than I think.*

That whisper grew louder a year later when I decided to take on the Twin Cities Marathon. It felt impossible, too big, but I signed up anyway. For nine months, I started small, running just a little longer each week, and gave everything I had. I ran through rain, exhaustion, and the taste of electrolyte goo that can only be described as regret in a packet. My longest training run was twenty miles, and when I finished, I thought, *I can do this.*

A week before the marathon, I twisted my ankle in a pothole. The doctor said I could still run but warned, "It's going to hurt." He wasn't wrong.

On race day, the biting 37-degree cold sank into my bones. By mile twenty, my legs felt like they didn't belong to me, and every step sent pain shooting through my body. A medic gently asked, "Do you want to ride the golf cart and be done?" It took everything in me not to say yes. Doubt flooded in: *Why did I think I could do this? What was I trying to prove?*

But then came another whisper: *Keep going.* Step by agonizing step, I refused to give up. When I crossed the finish line, tears were streaming down my face as I heard my name called over the loudspeaker: "Sam Eaton, 4:41:26." It was more than the end of a race; it was a declaration: *I am capable of more than I ever believed.*

Big dreams will test you. They'll stretch, challenge, and force you to face your fears head-on. But they'll also uncover strength you didn't know you had. Sometimes the path to courageous growth starts with chasing something that scares you—something so big that it feels like failure is a real possibility. That's when you discover what you're truly made of.

I'm not saying you need to run a marathon. (Believe me, it was miserable.) But maybe it's time to dream a big, bold dream again. Perhaps it's time to take that leap and prove that you're capable of far more than you ever imagined.

RECKLESSLY ALIVE AFFIRMATION

I AM STRONGER THAN MY DOUBTS, AND EVERY STEP FORWARD HELPS BUILD A LIFE I'M PROUD OF.

REFLECTION

What's a dream or goal you've been putting off because it feels too big or too scary? What's one small step you can take to help you move forward?

You can do this.

REWRITE YOUR INNER VOICE

I USED TO THINK AFFIRMATIONS WERE RIDICULOUS—THE KINDS of things you'd see in a rom-com where the main character chants, "I am strong; I am confident," in the mirror, only to trip over their own feet moments later. Affirmations often feel forced, awkward, and cringey. But they aren't about magic or pretending. They're about practice.

Think of these positive messages as a reset button for the inner dialogue that, for most of us, typically runs on autopilot. Our minds often replay the same doubts and criticisms we've picked up over the years. Affirmations interrupt that loop and rewrite the script.

You might say, "I can handle hard things," but then wonder, *Who am I kidding?* That's okay. Change and courageous growth rarely feel comfortable at first. Here's how to start changing your inner voice with affirmations:

1. **Find words that resonate.** Begin with what feels real. Maybe it's, *I'm trying my best today*, or, *I am stronger than my challenges.*
2. **Speak like you believe them.** Say them aloud, even if it feels awkward. Speak with the kindness you'd offer a friend.

3. **Put them where you'll see them.** Write them down on sticky notes, in phone reminders, or in a notebook. Look at them often.
4. **Repeat until familiar.** Repetition is key. Practice daily, especially when life feels heavy.

Affirmations aren't about pretending everything is fine. They're about creating a steady voice that reminds you of your worth. When the unexpected happens, and it will, you won't face it empty-handed. You'll have an anchor, a voice that steadies you in the storm and whispers, *I've got this. I am capable, I am worthy, and I am enough.*

RECKLESSLY ALIVE AFFIRMATION

I AM CAPABLE. I AM WORTHY. I AM ENOUGH.

REFLECTION

Think about an unexpected challenge you've faced recently. How did your inner voice respond in that moment? What words of encouragement could you have used at that time? How can you start speaking them to yourself today?

You can do this.

DAY 10

REDEFINE YOUR WORTH

FOR A LONG TIME, I BELIEVED THAT ACHIEVING MORE WOULD make me feel worthy. I worked tirelessly, chasing perfection and pouring everything I had into earning approval from others. I thought if I could accomplish the next thing—win the award, get the promotion, hit the goal—I'd finally silence the voice in my head that said, *I'm not enough*.

But no matter how much I achieved, it was never enough. The finish line kept moving, and the applause was fleeting. That forced me to confront a painful truth: Tying my worth to my achievements was a trap. Because if your worth depends on your success, it also disappears in the face of failure.

Your worth isn't a prize to be won. It's not something you earn by doing enough or achieving enough. It's something that's already inside you. Believing in your worth, no matter what happens, is an act of courageous growth—a decision to honor who you are over what you accomplish.

It took time, but I've learned to stop chasing my *enoughness* and start believing that it's already mine. That doesn't mean I don't celebrate accomplishments or set big goals. I just don't let them define me. Success and failure may be a part of my journey, but they don't decide my value.

So if you're feeling the weight of expectation today, let me remind you that your worth is not conditional. Whether you soar or stumble, your worth remains constant. You are enough—not because of what you achieve but because you exist.

The most valuable things you'll ever have aren't the trophies, titles, or accolades; they're the moments you show up as your authentic self, loving, growing, and making the world better in ways only you can. You don't have to achieve anything today. Trust that your greatest achievements are not in what you do but in the person you're becoming along the way.

RECKLESSLY ALIVE AFFIRMATION

I AM WORTHY AND ENOUGH, EXACTLY AS I AM.

REFLECTION

How have you measured your worth in the past? What could change if you genuinely believed that your worth is steady and unshakable, no matter what happens?

You can do this.

DAY 11

Resilience

SEE REJECTION AS REDIRECTION

IN MY MID-TWENTIES, I THOUGHT MY DREAM JOB HAD LANDED IN my lap. My best friend called with the opportunity we'd fantasized about during countless late nights in the college library—a chance to work together as codirectors for a major organization. It felt too good to be true. I applied, made it to the final two candidates, and gave everything I had in the interview.

But throughout the process, a tiny voice in my mind whispered doubts. Something about the culture didn't sit right, but I brushed it off. After all, this was the job we'd always talked about, wasn't it?

When the call came saying they'd chosen the other candidate, I collapsed onto my bed and cried. The sting of rejection felt like it would break me. I'd poured my heart into that opportunity, and it still wasn't enough. At the time, it felt like a catastrophic failure. The rejection burrowed into my mind, pulling up memories of every other time I'd fallen short.

In the following years, I learned that the job I'd been so crushed to lose was part of a toxic environment. My friend left his position there not long after, confirming what my gut had tried to tell me. Losing that opportunity turned out to be the best thing that could have happened. It cleared the path for me to step into the work I do now, work that fills my days with purpose and joy.

Rejection stings; there's no sugarcoating it. It feels personal, painful, and final. But choosing to see rejection as redirection is an act of courageous growth. It doesn't mean you won't grieve the dreams that didn't unfold as you had hoped. But when you see rejection as redirection, it softens the edges. It reminds you that every closed door directs your next step toward something better than you ever imagined.

RECKLESSLY ALIVE AFFIRMATION

I TRUST THAT REJECTION CAN LEAD ME TO SOMETHING BETTER. I AM BEING GUIDED TO THE RIGHT PATH.

REFLECTION

Think about a time when a rejection led you to something unexpected—something better. How might this perspective change how you view a past or current "no"?

You can do this.

ASK FOR HELP

SELF-CARE ONCE FELT LIKE SOMETHING I HAD TO HANDLE IN ISOlation—as if pulling myself together were a test I had to pass on my own. Asking for help? That felt like admitting I'd failed. If I couldn't get something done, I thought pushing harder was the answer.

Despite my stubborn independence, I've learned that some of the most powerful self-care isn't something you do alone. It's asking for help when you're stuck. It's letting someone hold you accountable for the thing you keep putting off or can't seem to tackle on your own. It's realizing that self-care doesn't always mean a solo recharge; it can also mean opening up and letting someone else into your struggle.

Maybe it's asking a friend to check in about the project you've been procrastinating. Perhaps it's setting up a session with a coach, therapist, or mentor who can help you untangle the mental knots holding you back. Maybe it's as simple as texting someone, "Hey, I need help staying on track this week. Can you check in on me?"

Asking for help doesn't make you weak. It's a sign of courageous growth: a step toward building the life you want instead of staying stuck in cycles of frustration. At times, the biggest act of self-care isn't checking off everything on your to-do list; it's admitting you can't do it all alone. When you let people into your process, you create space for momentum. You take the weight off your shoulders and allow others to help you carry it.

So if you're staring down something you've been avoiding, whether it's a goal, a tough conversation, or a change you know you need to make, ask for help. Accountability and support aren't weaknesses; they're lifelines. And the truth is, we were never meant to do this life alone.

You are worthy of care, connection, and support, and it starts with the courage to ask for what you need.

RECKLESSLY ALIVE AFFIRMATION

I AM NOT ALONE IN MY JOURNEY. ASKING FOR HELP IS A STRENGTH THAT FUELS MY GROWTH AND MOMENTUM.

REFLECTION

Think about a task, goal, or challenge you've been avoiding. What's holding you back from tackling it? Who in your life could you turn to for support or accountability? Reflect on how asking for help might make this process feel less overwhelming and more achievable.

You can do this.

REIMAGINE YOUR LIFE

I USED TO FEEL LIKE I WAS SUFFOCATING UNDER THE WEIGHT OF my own life. Have you ever felt that way? Wake up, work, pay bills, sleep, repeat. The same routines, the same coffee mug, the same gray sky outside the window. Every day blurred into the next, like a treadmill I couldn't escape. I kept asking myself, *Is this all there is? What's the point of any of this?*

I wasn't looking for a constant state of happiness. I just wanted my life to feel like it mattered, to find purpose beyond the endless cycle of tasks and to-do lists. But nothing seemed to change, and monotony crept in. One day I looked around and realized that I felt completely stuck.

For a long time, I thought purpose had to be something grand, like selling all my possessions and moving to Guam to "find myself." But maybe purpose isn't always about uprooting your life or chasing some life-altering dream. Perhaps it can be about reimagining the life you already have and finding the courage to live with so much purpose and energy that it helps the people around you feel more alive too. Maybe it's about showing up for the ordinary moments, infusing them with joy, and letting them add up to something extraordinary over time.

For me, that started with small, silly steps. I danced badly to ridiculous playlists while washing dishes—but with enthusiasm. I ordered the octopus appetizer at a restaurant just to say I had.

I joined a hip-hop dance class where I didn't know a soul and looked like a fool.

If you feel stuck, maybe the answer isn't waiting for a perfect plan. Perhaps it's asking yourself, *How can I make this moment feel more alive?*

I hope you'll lean in to the little moments of joy and whimsy today. Courageous growth isn't about reaching a destination; it's about living more fully right where you are.

RECKLESSLY ALIVE AFFIRMATION

I CAN CREATE PURPOSE, ONE SMALL, JOYFUL CHOICE AT A TIME.

REFLECTION

What's one small thing you can do today to make an ordinary moment feel more alive? How might your perspective shift if you saw purpose not as a destination but as something you create in the way you live your everyday life?

You can do this.

THE COURAGE TO CONNECT

I'VE KNOWN SEASONS OF HEAVINESS THAT WERE HARD TO PUT into words, times that felt unbearably lonely. Unfortunately, maybe you can relate. For me, the absence of connection has been one of the most painful experiences—like carrying an invisible weight no one else can see.

My brain has a way of clinging to the negative, circling the places where my relationship feels broken, and getting stuck in sadness. This cycle is easy to fall into and hard to escape, especially when disconnection is everywhere. Waiting for someone else to bridge the gap only makes the ache worse.

One of the most powerful shifts I've learned is to extend my hand first. Connection doesn't have to start with something big; it can begin with a small act, like offering a compliment, sending a kind message, or taking the risk to reach out. These moments may feel insignificant, but they can cut through the heaviness and remind us that we're not alone.

Connection isn't about elaborate plans or perfect circumstances. It's about presence, the consistent ways we show up for one another and remind us that we're seen and valued. It might be a genuine conversation, a shared laugh, or simply sitting with someone through challenging moments. These small acts create a ripple of belonging, one interaction at a time, and they matter more than we often realize.

Courageous growth means stepping into that space, even when loneliness tempts you to retreat. It's about taking a step toward someone else—not because it's easy but because it's how we rediscover our place in the world and remind others of theirs.

Connection is what gives life its depth and meaning. If you're feeling lonely, take a step. Reach out, notice someone, or let someone notice you. These moments don't only create connection, but they also remind you of your strength and your ability to help others feel seen. And on days that seem especially difficult, they can be enough to begin breaking the cycle of loneliness and finding your way back to belonging.

RECKLESSLY ALIVE AFFIRMATION

I AM BRAVE ENOUGH TO REACH OUT AND CREATE CONNECTION.

REFLECTION

Where can you create a small moment of connection today? Is there someone you can reach out to, a kindness you can offer, or a way to be fully present with the people around you?

You can do this.

WEEK 3

EMBRACING THE UNEXPECTED

THIS WEEK IS ABOUT STEPPING INTO THE UNKNOWN AND EMBRACING the unexpected moments that shape our lives. Whether we say yes to an unplanned opportunity, rethink how we speak to ourselves, celebrate the paths we've chosen (or those we've left behind), or take small steps toward purpose and connection, life often unfolds unexpectedly.

Each step will guide us toward finding meaning in the detours and strength in the surprises. We discover new layers of resilience, self-worth, and connection by leaning in to uncertainty with courage, curiosity, and trust. Together, let's practice seeing the unexpected not as an obstacle but as an invitation to grow, heal, and become more fully ourselves.

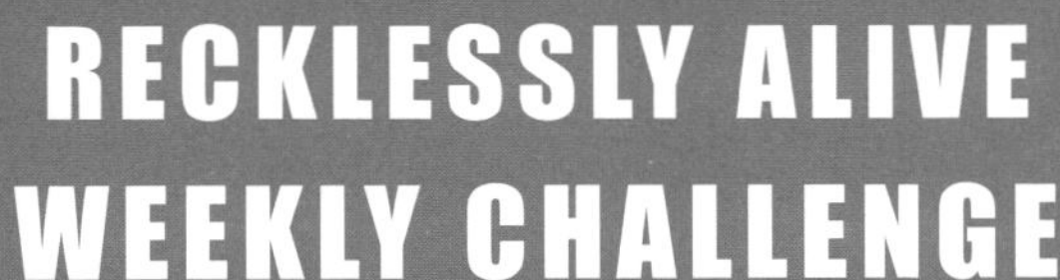

RECKLESSLY ALIVE WEEKLY CHALLENGE

Take one day this week to set aside your normal routine and leave space for the unexpected. Go for a drive with no destination, explore an old bookstore, or leave an hour unscheduled and see where it takes you. Reflect on what you notice or discover when you let go of the plan.

EMBRACE THE UNEXPECTED ADVENTURE

THREE DAYS AFTER SAYING YES TO A JOB I WAS WILDLY UNQUALIfied for, I was waking up at 5:30 a.m., pulling on a thick, green cotton uniform that smelled like it had spent a few decades in storage, and staring at myself in the mirror. I couldn't help but laugh. Was this really my life? A college kid from the suburbs suddenly turned Boy Scout camp archery director?

My summer wasn't supposed to be like this. The plan had been simple: Work a new job at a restaurant, save some money, and relax with my high school friends at the lake every possible moment. But on my first day, the restaurant manager greeted me with, "Oh, we forgot we hired you. We don't have any hours for you."

I could've sulked. I could've spent the summer binge-watching lousy reality TV and leaving one-star reviews on the restaurant's Yelp page from seventeen different email addresses. Instead, I posted online that I needed a job *fast*. An old classmate messaged me within hours, "Our archery director has quit. Come work at Boy Scout camp!"

Here's the thing: I wasn't a Boy Scout and certainly wasn't outdoorsy. The idea of me teaching archery to kids was absurd; I'd never even held a bow before. But the more I thought about it, the more it felt like an adventure.

Upon arriving at camp, I spent one whirlwind weekend becoming a certified archery instructor before the campers arrived. Then, my days were spent sweating under the blazing sun, teaching kids how to shoot arrows, fielding their wide-eyed questions, and even organizing a funeral for an unlucky mouse that crossed paths with a wayward shot. Evenings were a blur of camp-wide games, off-key campfire songs, and bonding with coworkers over mosquito bites and charred marshmallows. By the end of July, much to my surprise, I was named Staff Member of the Month.

Looking back, that summer job wasn't just a way to make money; it was a crash course in embracing the unexpected. Saying yes to that opportunity gave me more than a paycheck; it gave me one of the best summers of my entire life. The unplanned moments often shape us the most and leave us with memories we'll treasure forever. And maybe today, a surprise detour could lead you somewhere better than you ever imagined.

RECKLESSLY ALIVE AFFIRMATION

I EMBRACE THE UNEXPECTED AND TRUST THAT
EACH STEP WILL LEAD ME TO BETTER DAYS.

REFLECTION

When was the last time life took an unexpected turn that ended up being better than what you had planned? What did it teach you about being open to detours?

You can do this.

DAY 16

THE UNEXPECTED VOICES THAT DEFINE US

FOR MOST OF MY TEENAGE YEARS, I DREAMED OF BECOMING A music teacher, hoping to inspire students the way my teachers had inspired me. Finding the best music college tucked away in the rolling valleys of Iowa felt like destiny, a place where I could finally turn my passion into purpose. So I went to music school.

But not everyone there saw my potential. "Are you stupid? Are you *that* stupid?" my voice professor said a few months into my training, his glare sharp enough to make me want to disappear. Week after week, his harsh words chipped away at the confidence I'd spent years building.

His voice became my own. *You're not good enough. You'll never make it.* I worked harder than ever, desperate to prove him wrong. But no matter what I did, it was never enough. Eventually he told me, "I don't want my name on your recital program. Find another teacher."

After a few tear-filled days, I found a new voice teacher. Twice a week, I showed up to her studio, head hung low, unsure if I'd ever feel capable again. Her encouragement was a balm to my wounds. With her belief in me, I started improving. Slowly, I realized that I had a choice: I didn't have to let one cruel voice diminish mine.

As I took the final bow at my senior recital, she met me backstage with a note. "I've never been prouder to have my name on someone's recital," it read. Tears filled my eyes as I hugged her, grateful for someone who had seen me, believed in me, and helped me find my voice again.

Embracing the unexpected opens doors to finding strength and growth in the detours. It's about refusing to let the voices of doubt—whether from others or ourselves—dictate our worth. Life will throw us off course, but sometimes those twists lead to a deeper understanding of who we are and what we're capable of.

As you learn to navigate those twists, the voices you allow into your life matter deeply. Surround yourself with voices that celebrate your victories, and speak to yourself with the kindness you deserve. The most important voice in your life will always be yours, so choose to let it guide you with love and belief.

RECKLESSLY ALIVE AFFIRMATION

I REFUSE TO LET CRUEL VOICES DEFINE ME.

REFLECTION

Who in your life believes in you? Who are your biggest fans? Are there voices you need to let go of in order to grow?

You can do this.

DAY 17

THE UNEXPECTED MIRROR

I WAS TWENTY-FOUR, STUCK IN MY FIRST "ADULT" JOB, AND DOING everything possible to blend in with the background. My self-worth was in shreds, unraveling with every sideways glance at coworkers who seemed more confident, more capable, more *everything.* Every mistake felt like proof that I didn't belong. I couldn't look in a mirror without hearing the voice in my head sneer, *Not good enough.* Instead of confronting this issue, I buried myself in endless tasks, hoping that if I stayed busy enough, I could ignore the gnawing ache of never feeling like I was enough.

One afternoon, while rushing out the office door, I overheard a coworker talking about me. He said to another colleague, "Man, that guy has such good energy. He was a fantastic hire."

I froze. *Good energy?* I figured it was a mistake or maybe some cruel office prank. But when I glanced back, they weren't laughing. They were talking like it was the most obvious thing in the world, like everyone else could see something I couldn't.

I carried those words like tiny pebbles in my pocket for days, turning them over in my mind. I started to notice the moments that felt like they aligned with that overheard version of me: a new hire who asked for my help on their first day, a coworker who stayed late to vent about life while I listened, and the admin who always smiled extra wide when I walked in.

For so long, I'd been wrapped up in what I thought was

wrong with me that I couldn't see what was right. One overheard compliment felt like someone had handed me a mirror I didn't know I needed.

There are moments when life will surprise you, not with a failure or setback but with an unexpected glimpse of who you truly are. Perhaps someone will notice the parts of you that shine without you trying, the parts you're too busy to notice.

If you've been stuck in a loop of self-doubt, take a deep breath. Borrow someone else's eyes for a moment. Listen to the compliments that make you squirm, the ones you're quick to dismiss. There's truth in them, even if you're not ready to believe them yet. The energy you bring, the kindness you show, and the way you make people feel are the things that speak louder than anything you'll ever do. Every now and then, something as small as the unexpected compliment can remind you of what's been there all along.

RECKLESSLY ALIVE AFFIRMATION

MY ENERGY AND KINDNESS MAKE A DIFFERENCE, EVEN WHEN I CAN'T SEE IT.

REFLECTION

Think of a time when someone shared something positive about you that you hadn't seen in yourself. What did their words reveal to you? How might you practice noticing and appreciating those qualities in your daily life?

You can do this.

TRUST YOURSELF IN THE UNEXPECTED

YEARS AGO MY THERAPIST CHALLENGED ME TO WRITE DOWN everything I was worried about. I filled three full pages with fears—*three pages!*—and handed the papers to her, expecting validation for my overthinking. Instead, she smiled and said, "Great. Now put it away. Let's see how many of these happen."

A month later, I pulled out the list and was shocked. Not a single fear had come true. I'd spent countless hours spinning through worst-case scenarios that never existed.

That exercise taught me that anxiety thrives on the illusion of control. It convinces us that worrying is the key to avoiding pain or disappointment. But we can't prevent bad things from happening, and anxiety tricks us into living out fears before they even occur. Instead of protecting us, anxiety steals the present moment and keeps us trapped in fear.

Fighting anxiety doesn't happen overnight, but here are some small steps I've collected from my experiences in therapy to use when I'm struggling:

1. **Name your fears.** Write them down to see them.
2. **Challenge your thoughts.** Ask yourself, *Is this fear based in reality, or is it a story my mind is spinning?*

3. **Focus on what you can control.** Shift your energy toward small, actionable steps.
4. **Practice presence.** Anxiety pulls you into a future that doesn't exist. Use grounding techniques like taking a few deep breaths, noticing five things around you, feeling your feet firmly on the ground, or even eating a sour candy, to stay present.

Anxiety doesn't simply live in your head; it camps out in your chest, sets off alarms in your nervous system, and floods your mind with endless *what-ifs*. It tries to convince you that by worrying enough, you can prepare for anything life throws your way. But resilience isn't about predicting the future. It's about letting go of uncertainty and trusting that you can handle whatever comes next.

RECKLESSLY ALIVE AFFIRMATION

I TRUST IN MY ABILITY TO HANDLE WHATEVER COMES MY WAY AND EMBRACE THE UNEXPECTED WITH COURAGE AND GRACE.

REFLECTION

Think about a time when anxiety convinced you the worst would happen. What unfolded? How might letting go of control and embracing the unexpected change how you approach your worries today?

You can do this.

DAY 19

THE UNEXPECTED MOMENTS TO CARE FOR YOURSELF

BETWEEN WORK, ERRANDS, FAMILY, AND THE ENDLESS TO-DO list, it's easy to tell yourself, *I'll rest when there's time.* But here's the truth: There's never time unless you make it.

Some seasons are so full that the long walks, journaling sessions, weekends away, or other things we picture when we think of self-care just aren't realistic. And that's okay too.

The beauty of self-care is that it doesn't require hours of solitude or a perfectly planned routine. It's about embracing the unexpected moments, those tiny pockets of space hidden in the noise, and letting them remind you to breathe, reset, and care for yourself.

It's a few deep inhales while your coffee brews. It's taking two minutes between meetings to step outside and let the sun warm your face. It's playing your favorite song on the drive home and allowing yourself to sing along, even if you're wildly off-key. It's saying no to one more commitment because your plate is already full.

When you start take the time to notice, these glimmers can start to bring you back to yourself: a smile from a stranger, a deep belly laugh, or a pause in your car.

Embracing the unexpected means being open to life's little

gifts, even when the day feels overwhelming. These moments might not fix everything, but they remind you that you don't have to wait for life to feel easier to find little sparks of happiness.

So today, instead of waiting for life to slow down, give yourself permission to pause. Even ten minutes can remind you that you're worthy of care, no matter how chaotic things seem. Those small moments aren't only acts of self-kindness—they're a way of saying, *I matter too.*

RECKLESSLY ALIVE AFFIRMATION

I AM OPEN TO THE SMALL, UNEXPECTED
MOMENTS OF CARE AND JOY.

REFLECTION

When was the last time you felt cared for in an unexpected way? How can you open yourself to those moments more often?

You can do this.

PURPOSE SHOWS UP IN THE UNEXPECTED

I'VE NEVER LOVED MY BIRTHDAY. OFTEN IT WAS A DAY MARKED BY disappointment and an underwhelming evening, reminding me about how forgettable I could be. A few years ago, the day was shaping up to be no different. I was returning from chaperoning a youth-group trip to the Wisconsin Dells water parks. Bad weather had cut our trip short, and with no plans waiting for me at home, the day stretched out like one big reminder of my unimportance.

On the bus ride home, I was slouched on my bench seat, staring at my phone, trying to distract myself from the ache creeping in. But then another chaperone, someone I barely knew, started chatting with me. Her voice was light, cheerful, and curious, so much so that I didn't mind talking back. Mid-conversation, she asked, "Wait . . . is today your birthday?" I nodded, a little embarrassed, and mumbled, "Yeah, but it's no big deal."

Her face lit up like she'd discovered I was secretly a rock star. "You're coming to my house tonight. No excuses!" she said. I stammered out a list of reasons why I couldn't, but she waved them off like a pro.

A few hours later, I was pulling into her driveway. Inside, her roommates greeted me with warm smiles, and there was a single cupcake with a candle waiting to be lit in the kitchen. They enthusiastically sang "Happy Birthday," not caring that I felt awkward and out of place. We spent the evening playing board games, laughing over ridiculous stories, and eating snacks that probably weren't meant to be dinner. The weight I'd been carrying all day lifted for a few hours.

That night she taught me that purpose isn't always about the plans we make or the grand goals we set. We often find it when we let go of control and choose to show up for someone else. It's about seeing a need, even a small one, and deciding to meet it.

If you feel you have no purpose, start by embracing the unexpected for someone else, like my new friend did for me. We didn't stay in touch; she moved away not long after that night, but she gave me something I'll never forget: one night of kindness when I needed it most. Though these small gestures may seem insignificant, they can mean the world to someone who needs them. And often, in those moments of caring for others, you'll find a renewed sense of purpose within yourself.

RECKLESSLY ALIVE AFFIRMATION

I WAS MADE ON PURPOSE, FOR A PURPOSE.

REFLECTION

Think about a time when someone unexpectedly made you feel seen or valued. How can you create that same kind of moment for someone else today?

You can do this.

FIND CONNECTION IN UNEXPECTED PLACES

THE COMMUNITY CENTER'S HEAVY DOORS CREAKED AS I STEPPED inside, my nerves jangling like the echoing footsteps in the hallway. My therapist had given me homework after weeks of isolating depression: Go to one social outing. Just one. I'd picked open-gym volleyball because it was something I used to enjoy. But as I stood there, gripping my water bottle like a life raft, my instinct was to bolt. Still, something deeper urged me to stay.

Preassembled teams laughed and joked inside the gym, their camaraderie punctuating how out of place I felt. I wandered around the center, rejected by group after group with, "Sorry, we're full." My last hope was a cluster of people standing awkwardly in a corner, avoiding eye contact. "Can I join you?" I asked. Someone shrugged, and I had a team just like that.

Our first games were comically bad. Balls hit the floor untouched, serves went wild, and miscommunication reigned supreme. We lost every match. Badly. My face burned with embarrassment, and I questioned why I'd come. Yet, as the games went on, something shifted.

When one teammate managed a lucky serve that clipped the net and landed in, we erupted in cheers. For the first time, we scored. The laughter and high fives cut through my loneliness like sunlight through heavy clouds. By the end, we weren't only losing less, we were also having fun. Something within me softened, and I felt connected for the first time in months.

Embracing the unexpected is a way to challenge the voice in your head that says, *Things will never get better.* It pushes back against the urge to retreat behind walls of self-protection, and it invites you to do the hard, brave thing: Try again, believe again, and open yourself to the possibility that connection and joy still exist, even when you can't see them.

So take a deep breath, and walk into something new. It may not be easy, and the first steps might feel awkward or uncomfortable—but they're worth it. Join a class, attend a group, or revisit an activity you used to enjoy. Most meaningful connections start with an awkward "hello" and grow through small, shared moments. Each step you take toward connection reminds you that you are worthy of belonging, and sometimes the courage to try again is all it takes to change everything.

RECKLESSLY ALIVE AFFIRMATION

I AM BRAVE ENOUGH TO TRY AGAIN, TO HOPE AGAIN, AND TO BELIEVE IN THE POSSIBILITY OF CONNECTION.

REFLECTION

What step can you take to connect or reconnect with others, even if it feels uncomfortable? How might embracing the unexpected bring light into areas of your life that feel heavy or stuck?

You can do this.

WEEK 4

THE SPACES THAT SHAPE US

THE SPACES WE LIVE IN—PHYSICALLY, EMOTIONALLY, AND mentally—play a huge role in who we are and how we present ourselves to the world. These spaces hold our routines and stories, along with the tiny moments when we grow without even realizing it. When we start to pay attention to how our environments affect us, we can shape them to support who we're trying to become.

This week, we'll reflect on the environments that have shaped us, whether it's the physical places we call home, the people we surround ourselves with, or the mindsets we carry. Some spaces push us forward; others hold us back. By choosing where we invest our energy, we create the momentum to live a life we're proud of. Let's step into this week with intention, ready to shape the spaces that shape us.

RECKLESSLY ALIVE WEEKLY CHALLENGE

Set a timer and clean or declutter for ten minutes one day this week. Focus on one small area of your physical or digital environment. When the timer goes off, if you want to be done, stop. And if you have the energy to keep going, lean in to that momentum. Even a small reset can shift your energy. Let this be a simple win, a reminder that you have the power to create change, right where you are.

CREATING PEACE IN OUR SPACES

WHEN I'M NOT AT MY BEST, MY SPACE SHOWS IT. DISHES SIT IN the sink, their faint smell fighting with the mystery leftovers in the fridge. Clothes pile up in corners, turning into small mountains of procrastination. Unopened mail plus random odds and ends clutter surfaces that were once clean and calm.

My surroundings reflect my mind, scattered, heavy, and out of control. The worst part? When I'm overwhelmed, I don't have the energy to tackle the mess. The clutter becomes louder, the chaos is more suffocating, and the room feels like it's echoing, *See? You can't even handle* this.

But here's what I'm learning: Our worth isn't tied to the state of our space. It's okay if your home doesn't look like it's straight out of a magazine. Life can be challenging, and getting through the day is enough.

The spaces that shape us don't need to be perfect in order to support us. When I find the energy to make a move, I remind myself that it doesn't all have to be fixed in one go. I start small. Maybe it's clearing the kitchen table so I can eat without balancing my plate on my lap. Or tossing the laundry into a basket, even if it hasn't made it to the washer yet.

When everything feels overwhelming, the key is to build

momentum. Break down the biggest tasks into manageable steps. It's not about transforming your entire space in one day or meeting some unrealistic standard. It's about choosing one thing, no matter how small, that moves you toward calm rather than chaos.

Every small act of care sends a powerful message to yourself: *I'm showing up. I'm capable. I'm doing what I can.*

RECKLESSLY ALIVE AFFIRMATION

EVEN SMALL STEPS MATTER, AND I AM
WORTHY OF CARE, NO MATTER WHAT.

REFLECTION

What's one space in your life, physical or digital, that's been feeling a little overwhelming? What's one small thing you could do today to bring more peace or clarity to that space?

You can do this.

Self-Talk 

THE VOICES THAT SHAPE US

THE FIRST TIME I ENTERED A CROSSFIT GYM, I WAS SO NERVOUS that my palms became slick with sweat. I wasn't an athletic kid, and I'd never lifted a weight in my life. And suddenly I found myself exercising alongside people who looked like they bench-pressed trucks for fun. The air smelled like rubber mats and determination, and I half expected someone to tell me I'd wandered into the wrong building.

During one of my first workouts, I finished more than five minutes after everyone else in the group. I could feel my face burning with embarrassment as I willed my body to keep moving, certain I'd hear snide comments or see someone smirk as I struggled through the final reps. But none of that happened. Instead, every single person stayed to cheer me on, shouting, "You've got this!" and clapping until I finished. It was more than encouraging; it was transformative.

Months later, I was traveling and decided to attempt a workout on my own. Halfway through, struggling to keep going, I realized something that made me stop mid-rep: The voice in my head wasn't my usual critic, whispering that I wasn't good enough. Instead, I heard my coach's steady encouragement. I heard my gym friends cheering me on, even though they were miles away.

It made me think about the spaces that shape us, not only

physical spaces but also the people and voices that fill them. Who are the voices shaping how we see ourselves? Are they lifting us up, reminding us we're capable, strong, and worthy? Or are they adding to the self-doubt that's already hard enough to shake?

If you're noticing that the voices around you aren't the ones you need, it's okay to step back. It's okay to be intentional about who gets a say in your life because the way you talk to yourself often echoes the people closest to you. Surround yourself with voices that build you up, and over time you'll start hearing their voices in your head when you need them most.

Never forget that you have the power to be that voice for someone else too. Every word of encouragement and each moment you choose to see someone's potential instead of their shortcomings matters. Whether it's in a gym, at work, or in your everyday relationships, you can help create a space where people feel seen, supported, and reminded of their worth.

RECKLESSLY ALIVE AFFIRMATION

I CHOOSE TO SURROUND MYSELF WITH PEOPLE
WHO SEE AND CELEBRATE MY WORTH.

REFLECTION

Who are the voices that shape how you see yourself? How do you feel after spending time with the people closest to you? What's one step you can take to spend more time with those who uplift and encourage you?

You can do this.

RECLAIM YOUR DIGITAL SPACE

THE NOTIFICATION PINGED, BREAKING THE PEACE OF MY EVENING. *One quick scroll*, I told myself. Fifteen minutes later, I was still glued to my phone, lost in a sea of polished vacation photos, impossibly clean kitchens, and people who seemed to have life figured out. The pizza on my plate had gone lukewarm, and my mind was berating me, *Why am I not doing more? Why don't I look like that? Why does everyone else seem so much farther ahead?*

I hadn't started the night feeling inadequate, but somehow that's where I'd landed. My cozy apartment suddenly felt smaller, my to-do list heavier, and my mood, well, somewhere south of inspired. I wasn't simply scrolling; I was letting my online world shape my view of myself.

That night, as I plugged in my phone to charge, I made a vow: This wouldn't be my norm. If my digital space had that much power over me, I needed to take some of it back.

The next day, I sat down with a clear mission: Unfollow anything that chipped away at my worth. The endless highlight reels of perfection? Gone. The accounts that left me feeling "less than"? Muted. In their place, I sought out voices that felt real, people who shared their struggles, celebrated small wins, and weren't afraid to be messy.

It wasn't only about who I followed; it was about how I used my time. I set new rules: no endless scrolling before bed, no reaching for my phone before coffee, and a daily break from the constant pull of notifications. Slowly, my digital world started to change. The noise subsided. My feed became a place that inspired me rather than draining me.

The spaces that shape us aren't limited to where we live or work. They're in the screens we stare at, the voices we let in, and the messages we absorb without realizing it. If your online world feels heavy, know this: You have the power to make it lighter.

Your worth isn't determined by likes or followers or curated perfection. It's rooted in who you are, not in what you consume. Take back your space. Reclaim your peace. And remember: The world beyond the screen is waiting for you.

RECKLESSLY ALIVE AFFIRMATION

MY WORTH DOES NOT COME FROM A SCREEN.

REFLECTION

How does my current digital environment make me feel? What's one step I can take today to reclaim my online space and protect my peace?

You can do this.

Resilience 

THE POWER OF INSPIRING SPACES

WHEN I FIRST STARTED MY BUSINESS, I THOUGHT WORKING FROM home would be the dream. No commute, no dress code, just me, my big ideas, and endless possibilities. But the truth? My days blurred together, consumed by distractions and a constant stream of self-doubt. I couldn't focus, couldn't find the motivation. The more I tried to power through, the more overwhelmed I became. Every unfinished task on my desk seemed to scream, *You're not cut out for this!* It wasn't just the mess in my space; it was the mess in my head.

Then, someone mentioned a coworking space in town—a bright, open office where people were working to make the world a better place, each in their own way. At first, I hesitated. It felt intimidating, like I was stepping into a club where everyone else belonged and had their life figured out. But eventually, I packed up my laptop and gave it a shot.

Walking in, I was hit with the buzz of quiet energy. Natural light spilled across rows of desks, plants softened the edges of the space, and the walls were dotted with colorful art. The people weren't intimidating at all. They were kind and outgoing, sharing stories of their work over lunch. One was launching a nonprofit for foster kids. Another was building an app to reduce food waste. Their passion and purpose were contagious, and I found myself thinking, *I want to do my part too.*

Something shifted that day. Suddenly I felt more resilient in the face of unfinished projects and big dreams. It wasn't because I'd miraculously found better work habits or become a genius overnight. It was the space. The energy, the community, and the inspiration all made it easier to rise to the challenges of entrepreneurship. All it took was a change of scene.

The spaces that shape us matter. They don't erase the hard parts of life, but they make them more manageable. Lean in to the environments that inspire you. Seek out spaces where you feel supported, connected, and encouraged. We don't always feel resilient, but that isn't because we are weak. It's because we haven't found a space that supports us, one that doesn't require us to carry the weight alone. If that's where you are, pause for a moment and notice what's already within reach.

RECKLESSLY ALIVE AFFIRMATION

I CHOOSE TO SURROUND MYSELF WITH SPACES THAT ENCOURAGE GROWTH AND RESILIENCE.

REFLECTION

Which spaces in your life make it easier to stay resilient? How can you spend more time in places that inspire and uplift you?

You can do this.

FIND WAYS OUT OF A TOXIC SPACE

THE CANDLES WERE LIT, THE SOFT MUSIC WAS PLAYING, AND I had convinced myself that lavender essential oil could fix everything. Yet, no matter how many affirmations I whispered or journals I filled, the weight of being in a harmful environment didn't lift.

I thought I could out-journal the stress, out-breathe the tension, and out-yoga the exhaustion. But it wasn't until my therapist gently said, "I'm not sure you'll be able to heal while you still work there," that the truth I'd been avoiding finally hit me: No amount of soothing rituals could undo the damage of being in a place that sucked the life out of me.

It's true that certain practices can help us cope, but they can't heal everything. It's like trying to plant flowers in poisoned soil. They might show little signs of life for a while, but eventually the environment takes over. Often, the most radical act of care isn't another bath or meditation; it's planning a way out.

I know how hard it is. When the situation is tied to a paycheck, a relationship, or a family dynamic that feels impossible to change, it's easy to feel trapped. I've been there, staring at a reality that seemed like it would never shift.

But if you find yourself in an environment where you feel

like you can't thrive, use some of your self-care time to help move you toward a new beginning. The spaces that shape us—where we work, live, and gather—have a profound impact on our well-being. It's not selfish to seek out something better. Changing our environment can be one of the most powerful forms of self-love and self-care that we have access to.

RECKLESSLY ALIVE AFFIRMATION

I AM WORTHY OF A SPACE THAT NURTURES
MY GROWTH AND PEACE.

REFLECTION

How are your current environments impacting your well-being? What is one step you can take today, big or small, to move closer to a space that supports your growth and peace?

You can do this.

DAY 27

THE SPACES THAT RESTORE US

LIFE GETS NOISY. DEADLINES PILE UP LIKE A TEETERING JENGA tower. Notifications buzz incessantly, each one a different demand that claws at your attention. In all that chaos, it's easy to lose the voice inside, the one whispering your purpose and reminding you why you're here.

But when you step outside into nature, the world slows down. The sky stretches wide without hurrying. Trees don't rush to grow; they stand rooted, patient, stretching toward the light. Rivers carve their paths with persistence, reminding us that purpose isn't always about speed but also about steady, deliberate movement. Nature has a rhythm that feels ancient and grounding, gently inviting us to reconnect with our own.

In nature, there's no pressure to perform, no expectation to have it all figured out. It offers its presence freely, asking nothing in return. And when you let it work on you, something shifts. The problems that seemed overwhelming begin to shrink. The seasons teach you that growth isn't constant or linear and that rest, patience, and stillness are part of the process too. Purpose doesn't always arrive in grand epiphanies; purpose often reveals itself in the moments when we finally make space to listen.

When life feels heavy, let nature be one of the spaces that

shapes you. Let the stars whisper your place in the vastness, the wind thread through your tangled thoughts, and the solid ground beneath your feet remind you that you belong.

Some days, the best way to rediscover your purpose is to step outside and let the vast, beautiful world remind you of who you are and who you're meant to be.

RECKLESSLY ALIVE AFFIRMATION

IN THE STILLNESS,
I REMEMBER WHO I AM AND WHY I AM HERE.

REFLECTION

How can spending time in nature help you reconnect with what matters most? Where do you feel most alive with wonder and calm?

You can do this.

DAY 28

THE SPACES THAT BRING US TOGETHER

WE TELL OURSELVES THAT CONNECTION CAN WAIT UNTIL OUR spaces are perfect. Once the dishes are done, the laundry is folded, and the couch pillows are arranged, we'll open our door, make the call, or invite someone in. But that version of perfect? It's a moving target. The special people in your life overlook the dishes in the sink or the clutter on the counter. They care about *you*.

Believing that our spaces need to be flawless holds us back. We hesitate to invite others into our lives, afraid they'll judge the mess or see through the cracks in the image we'd like to present, the difference between what we'd like it to be and what it is. But connection isn't born from perfection. It's built in the moments when we let down our guard and allow others to see us as we are.

Think about how someone else's imperfect space has made you feel at home. Mismatched cups of coffee shared around a messy kitchen table. Hours of good conversation on a friend's tattered and stained couch. These moments stand out because they feel real. They remind us that connection isn't about a spotless home; it's about being present, about showing up.

When we focus too much on appearances, we miss opportunities for a deeper connection. Let's make the spaces that shape us ones that foster belonging. A friend who needs your support doesn't care if your floor is vacuumed; they care that you answer the phone. The people who matter aren't expecting you to have it all together; they're looking for authenticity, and more than anything, they're looking for you.

So the next time you find yourself hesitating, let the moment be enough. Invite someone over, even if the laundry isn't done. Share a meal, even if it's takeout straight from the box. Let connection happen in the middle of your real, messy life.

Perfection isn't a prerequisite for love or friendship. The beauty of connection is that it thrives not in polished spaces but in genuine ones. Open your door, your heart, and your life as they are and let true connection meet you where you're at.

RECKLESSLY ALIVE AFFIRMATION

CONNECTION STARTS WHEN I STOP HIDING AND LET PEOPLE SEE MY AUTHENTIC SELF.

REFLECTION

What space in your life feels most connected to others, and why? What's one simple way to create more space for connection this week?

You can do this.

WEEK 5

BREAKING FREE FROM WHAT'S HOLDING YOU BACK

THERE ARE MOMENTS IN LIFE WHEN IT FEELS LIKE WE HAVE TO carry more than we can hold. Whether it's the weight of past mistakes, the pressure of others' opinions, or the overwhelming grind of daily life, we can easily start to feel overloaded. We start to believe lies that tell us we're trapped, that change is out of reach, and that the life we want is slipping farther away. But the truth? You have more power than you think. Breaking free isn't about a sweeping moment of courage; it's about a series of bold, intentional choices that shift your trajectory over time.

This week, we'll explore what it means to loosen the grip of the things that hold us back. From redefining self-worth to finding resilience in the face of criticism, the focus of this week is about reclaiming your agency. It's about recognizing that the barriers between you and the life you want aren't unmovable. You don't have to stay stuck, and you don't have to have it all figured out. The first step is believing that change is possible, and then taking the next step, no matter how small, toward a freer, fuller life.

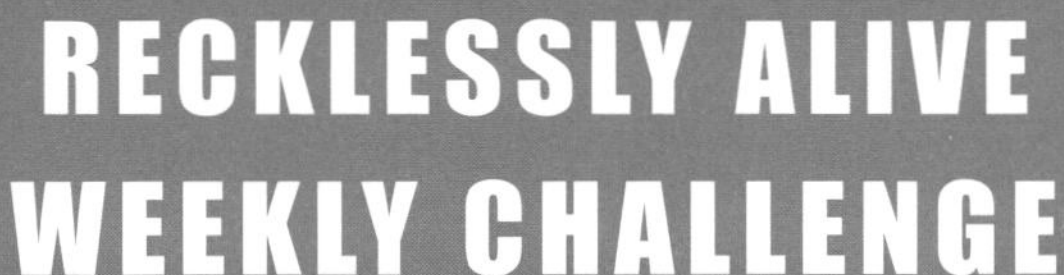

Identify one area of your life where you feel stuck or weighed down. What's one small, actionable step you can take this week to create momentum? Whether it's having a difficult conversation, decluttering a space, or trying something new, take that step as a reminder that you can do this. Celebrate the courage it takes to move forward.

BREAK FREE FROM WHAT FEELS IMPOSSIBLE

AT TWENTY-FIVE, I WAS BURIED UNDER $90,000 OF STUDENT LOAN debt. My teacher's salary of $40,000 barely covered the basics, and the unopened bills on my desk were a constant reminder of how far I felt from freedom. Every time I swiped my debit card, I felt guilt and shame, wondering, *How did I let it get this bad? Will I ever get out of debt?*

One night, as I stared at the pile of bills, I realized that nothing would change unless I did. I didn't have a perfect plan or even a lot of hope but simply the determination to start. I made uncomfortable choices. I swapped my smartphone for a flip phone to save over $100 a month, got strict with my grocery budget, and stopped saying yes to anything that didn't align with my goals. Each "maybe next time" to friends was hard, but I held on to the idea of a future where "next time" could be brighter.

I worked every extra job I could find, from tutoring to deejaying events, and sacrificed evenings and weekends. I studied everything I could about budgeting and debt payoff, finding encouragement in the stories of others who had done the same. Slowly, I started to see progress. Each payment wasn't only a step toward becoming debt-free; it was proof that I could do this.

Four years later, I made my final payment. The relief was

overwhelming. The weight I'd carried for so long was finally gone, and I felt peace for the first time in years.

Breaking free from what's holding you back starts with facing it head-on. Sacrifice isn't glamorous or popular. Our world thrives on quick fixes and instant gratification, but real transformation requires something deeper. It demands consistency, discomfort, and the courage to move forward when every part of you wants to quit.

Keep going, even when it's hard, even when you don't see the finish line yet. Because every deliberate choice you make is a step closer to the life you've been dreaming of, and I promise, the freedom will be worth it.

RECKLESSLY ALIVE AFFIRMATION

I HAVE THE STRENGTH TO CREATE A LIFE
OF FREEDOM AND POSSIBILITY.

REFLECTION

What's one area of your life that's been weighing you down? What's a small, doable step you can take this week to remind yourself that change is possible?

You can do this.

DAY 30

BREAK FREE FROM FALSE NARRATIVES

THE TEXT MESSAGE I HAD SENT SAT THERE, UNREAD, WHILE MY mind raced into overdrive. *Are they mad at me? Did I say something wrong?* I mentally replayed every interaction from the past week, scrutinizing my words for anything that might have landed badly. *Did my joke fall flat? Was my last reply too short?* The silence wasn't simply silence anymore—it was a blank canvas that my brain eagerly painted with worst-case scenarios.

By the time my therapist's words floated into my mind, my heart was pounding. "What is another perspective?" she always asks. At that moment, another perspective felt impossible to find. But as I stared at my phone, I realized that there were countless explanations that had nothing to do with me. Maybe their phone had died. Perhaps they were caught up at work. Maybe they were binge-watching their favorite show and had lost track of time. The only certainty? My imagination wasn't doing me any favors.

Our minds are powerful storytellers, often crafting narratives out of thin air. My brain had turned silence into rejection, blame, and a problem that might not even exist. Breaking free from what's holding you back starts with recognizing these stories for what they are. The overthinking and inner dialogue that pull you into doubt don't have to define your reality. When you are spiraling, pause and ask, *What else could be true?*

This isn't about silencing your thoughts or ignoring your feelings; it's about questioning them. Anxiety convinces us that filling in the blanks is the only way to prepare for the worst, but it often leaves us tangled in fear and assumptions. What if you left space for grace instead? Silence isn't inherently bad. And even if there is an issue, trust that you can handle it when it comes. You don't need to carry the weight of every potential scenario before it unfolds.

Breaking free from the anxious self-talk that's holding you back takes practice, but it starts with small moments of curiosity and compassion. The next time your mind leaps to conclusions, take a deep breath and remind yourself that your first thought doesn't have to be the final word. You have the power to rewrite the story in your mind, create space for peace, and trust that everything will be okay.

RECKLESSLY ALIVE AFFIRMATION

I RELEASE ANXIOUS NARRATIVES AND TRUST
IN THE GOODNESS OF OTHERS.

REFLECTION

Where in your life are you assuming the worst? How can you challenge that story with another perspective today?

You can do this.

DAY 31

BREAK FREE FROM *SHOULD*

THE FIRST THING I FELT EVERY MORNING WASN'T THE WARMTH OF sunlight spilling through the curtains but the weight of *should*. Before my feet hit the floor, I was already beating myself up and feeling like I was behind.

I should've gone to bed earlier.
I should be doing more with my life.
I should have this figured out by now.

By the time I poured my coffee, the *should*s had taken over. Each sip tasted like failure; every thought circled back to what I wasn't doing, what I hadn't achieved, or where I'd fallen short. The worst part? *Should* always came with shame, whispering that I'd never measure up no matter how hard I tried.

On one of these days, I took a walk to clear my head. The crisp air bit at my cheeks, and the sound of leaves crunching underfoot gave me something solid to focus on as my mind spiraled through its usual loop: *I should be farther along in my career. I should have more money saved. I should feel happier.* Walking along, I started to focus on what *was*: the ground, the air, the trees. I started to breathe and look outward.

Breaking free from what's holding you back often starts with learning to see the *should*s for what they are: expectations you never agreed to. Who decides how far along you should be? Who's setting the deadline for when you should have everything figured out?

I realized that so many of these *should*s weren't even mine; they were echoes of comparisons I'd absorbed, standards I thought I had to meet to be worthy. But when I gave myself permission to put them down, I noticed something surprising. Without the weight of *should*, there was room to breathe, to feel proud of where I already was, and to dream about where I wanted to go—not because I should but because I *could*.

So today, try something radical. Question every *should* that tries to take up space in your mind. And then, dare to leave it behind.

RECKLESSLY ALIVE AFFIRMATION

I CHOOSE TO RELEASE THE *SHOULD*S AND EMBRACE THE FREEDOM TO LIVE ON MY OWN TERMS.

REFLECTION

What's one *should* that has been holding you back? How might your life change if you gave yourself permission to let it go?

You can do this.

BREAK FREE FROM OTHER OPINIONS

WHEN I WEIGHED 161 POUNDS, COWORKERS, ACQUAINTANCES, and people I thought were friends called me scrawny. "You need to eat more," they teased, their laughter cutting through me like the dull edge of a blade. When I packed on muscle and reached 195 pounds, those voices mocked me for being "too obsessed with fitness," scoffing at my carefully portioned meals.

When I was drowning in my mental health, those same people labeled me "too negative," their words stinging like salt in a wound I was already trying to heal. When I clawed my way back to feeling more like myself, others questioned, "Why is he so happy all the time?" as if contentment were something to distrust.

For years, I tied myself in knots trying to meet the world's shifting expectations, until one day, I stumbled on a truth that broke me and set me free: There's no winning their game. Some people, especially those who don't truly know you, will always find something negative to say.

So why not stop playing that game? Why not live a life that feels like yours—messy, brave, and unapologetically *your own*?

Breaking free from what's holding you back isn't about silencing others' negative voices; it's about refusing to let those voices shape you. It's about standing tall when they try to pull you down. It's about letting go of seeking their approval and reclaiming your choices, your voice, and your life.

Not everyone will understand you. Not everyone will celebrate your healing or cheer for your growth. And that's okay. You're the one who must live with your decisions, look at yourself in the mirror, and feel proud of the person looking back.

So let them talk. Let them misunderstand you. Their opinions aren't your truth. You don't need to carry the weight of their judgment. Instead, run toward the life that makes you feel fully and recklessly alive—because they will talk either way.

RECKLESSLY ALIVE AFFIRMATION

I WILL LIVE BOLDLY AS MYSELF, KNOWING THAT OTHERS DON'T GET TO WRITE MY STORY.

REFLECTION

Where have you been holding back because of someone else's opinion? What would you do differently if you let go of their judgment today?

You can do this.

BREAK FREE FROM AVOIDANCE

I DIDN'T PLAN TO SPEND MY EVENING SCROLLING THROUGH THE void of social media, but there I was, three hours deep, my dinner cold and untouched beside me, my thumb mindlessly swiping up, up, up. The notifications were long gone, but somehow I was still stuck in the loop, hypnotized by highlight reels, ridiculous memes, and a creeping sense of dissatisfaction. When I finally put the phone down, the room felt heavier, like the air had turned stale. This wasn't rest. It wasn't even fun. It was just noise, and I was letting it stop my life from feeling recklessly alive.

This wasn't the first time I'd mistaken distraction for self-care. Staying up late with Netflix left me feeling exhausted and not recharged. Overcommitting to plans I didn't enjoy drained my energy instead of filling my cup. I realized that I wasn't caring for myself. Instead, I was avoiding the discomfort of acknowledging what wasn't working.

True self-care asks more of us, not by masking discomfort with distractions but by addressing the habits that hold us back. It's choosing to go to therapy, even when it feels easier to avoid it. It's setting boundaries with people who drain you, even when guilt whispers that you shouldn't. It's drinking water, eating a real meal, and showing up for yourself in the ways you deserve, even when life feels overwhelming.

Breaking free from what's holding us back asks us to take

a hard look at the choices we make every day. Self-care doesn't always require doing more. One of the most healing things you can do is to release the habits and choices that keep pulling you under. That's how you reclaim your time, energy, and focus, by making space to pour them into the parts of your life that truly matter.

So today, instead of reaching for distractions that only add to the noise, be brave enough to pause. Ask yourself what you truly need. Because courageously letting go of what isn't helping is one of the most powerful things you can do.

RECKLESSLY ALIVE AFFIRMATION

I RELEASE WHAT NO LONGER SERVES ME AND CHOOSE THE CARE THAT NOURISHES MY SOUL.

REFLECTION

Which habits or distractions are weighing you down rather than helping you grow? How might letting go of them create space for something better? When you pause and ask yourself what you truly need, what comes to mind?

You can do this.

BREAK FREE BY PAYING IT FORWARD

I LOOKED OUT AT THE TWELVE INCREDIBLE YOUNG WOMEN IN front of me, their faces a mix of excitement and nerves, and felt the familiar tug of responsibility. These weren't simply soccer players; they were kids navigating the ups and downs of growing up, just like I had. At their age, I didn't believe that I mattered. I didn't think anyone truly saw me. But here I was, standing on the other side of that doubt, determined to make sure they knew how much they mattered.

Each practice became more than drills and scrimmages. In a hundred small ways, practice was an opportunity to tell them, "You belong here. You're seen." Whether it was celebrating their effort, listening when they opened up, or cheering them on from the sidelines, I wanted them to feel visible and valued. And each time I poured attention into them, I felt something shift in me, too, reminding me that my struggles had led me here, to this moment, where I could offer what I once needed.

Maybe that's what purpose looks like: taking the parts of your story that once felt heavy and letting them guide you to help someone else. It's seeing a piece of yourself in others and choosing to be the encouragement or support you once needed.

In those moments, your story becomes a lifeline, and in offering that hope, you find healing for yourself too.

Breaking free from what's holding you back can look like paying it forward, like reaching into a part of your story and putting love in motion to help someone standing in the ripple of your healing.

Your story, no matter how messy or painful, isn't over. Those difficult chapters you've lived through have shaped you into someone who can make a difference. Let your experiences remind you of how far you've come. Let them fuel your desire to show up for others. And let them prove that even the toughest chapters of life can lead to a deeper sense of connection and purpose. Just like on that soccer field, sometimes the most powerful thing we can do is remind someone they matter.

RECKLESSLY ALIVE AFFIRMATION

I AM TURNING MY HARDEST MOMENTS
INTO SOMETHING MEANINGFUL.

REFLECTION

Who in your life might need the encouragement or understanding you once needed? How can you show up for them this week?

You can do this.

BREAK FREE FROM PAST HURT

I SAT IN THE CORNER OF THE COFFEE SHOP, NURSING A LUKEWARM latte, my friend's words still ringing in my ears: "You've been distant lately." I wanted to defend myself, to say it wasn't true, but it was. I'd been pulling back, keeping her at arm's length without even realizing it. The truth was I didn't trust her, and it wasn't because of anything she'd done but because someone else had let me down years ago. I was waiting for her to hurt me, too, carrying that old betrayal into a friendship that didn't deserve it.

Breaking free from what's holding you back means recognizing when your past is creeping into your present. Those unhealed wounds, the ones we think we've left behind, have a way of whispering lies that tell us to guard our hearts, even when there's no real danger. That doesn't mean we forget the past, but we learn from it without letting it dictate the way we show up for new people.

Healing doesn't mean pretending the pain didn't happen. It asks that you acknowledge the hurt, learn the lessons it brought, and choose to let it shape you into someone stronger, not someone harder. Healing requires the courage to step out of the shadow of betrayal and into the light of connection, to trust a little more, even when fear tells you to run.

Not everyone will leave. Not everyone will betray you. And no one deserves to carry the blame for someone else's mistakes.

Letting go of those projections doesn't erase the scars; it transforms them into reminders of your resilience and your ability to grow.

The past has its place, but it doesn't belong in every relationship. You are free to hope again, to open yourself to the kind of love and connection that remind you of what's possible. The act of trusting isn't only a gift to others; it's also a gift to yourself, a declaration that you're no longer bound by what broke you. Your story is still unfolding, and the next chapter is yours to write.

RECKLESSLY ALIVE AFFIRMATION

I CHOOSE CONNECTION OVER FEAR.
MY PAST DOES NOT DEFINE MY RELATIONSHIPS TODAY.

REFLECTION

Where might old wounds be shaping how you show up in your relationships? How can you take one small step toward healing and trust today?

You can do this.

WEEK 6

RECLAIMING YOUR POWER

THERE ARE MOMENTS IN LIFE WHEN WE FEEL INSIGNIFICANT, when doubt whispers in our ears, the weight of circumstances pulls us down, and the voices around us make us question our place. In those times, it's easy to forget the strength within us and the courage waiting to rise. Reclaiming your power isn't about chasing an ideal or becoming someone new. It's about stripping away the noise and stepping back into who you've always been—the version of you that's bold, capable, and fully alive.

This week, we'll reconnect with that inner power. We'll explore how to take bold action when fear wants to keep you stuck, how to find resilience when the world feels heavy, and how to embrace your worth without apology.

Your power isn't something you have to seek from an outside source; it's already within you. Let's reclaim it together.

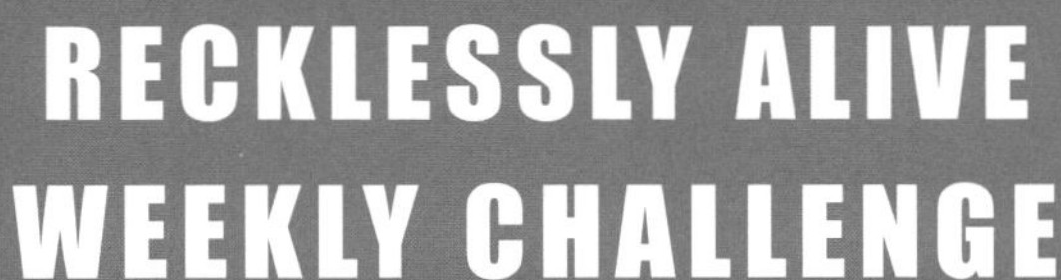

Identify one area of your life where you've been giving your power away through silence, self-doubt, or staying small. Take it back this week by speaking up, setting a boundary, or simply naming what you really want. Power returns when you stop asking permission to be fully yourself.

DAY 36

RECLAIM THE LIFE YOU WANT TO LIVE

MY FINGER HOVERED OVER THE MOUSE, THE CURSOR BLINKING ON the email that would change my life. My chest felt tight, and my stomach knotted with fear. *What if I fail? What if I can't support myself? What if this is the worst decision I'll ever make?*

For years, I worked as an elementary school music teacher. My days were a blend of squeaky recorders, kids' laughter, and the kind of beautiful chaos that only a classroom full of eight-year-olds can bring. I loved my students, but deep down a voice whispered, *There's something else you're meant to do.*

At first, I ignored it. I buried that voice under lesson plans and school concerts, convincing myself that I should be grateful for the life I had. But as I began writing my first book and speaking about mental health, the whisper grew louder. I didn't want to leave teaching, but I wasn't being honest with myself about what truly mattered. I had to ask, *What do I want my life to look like? What do I want most?*

The answer wasn't immediate, and the steps forward weren't easy. Often, reclaiming your power starts with listening to what matters most to you, even when it means stepping into uncertainty. For me, it took years of preparation, countless late nights, and an overwhelming amount of doubt. But the day I hit Send on my resignation email, I felt something I hadn't felt in years: freedom.

You don't have to quit your job or make a life-altering decision today, but you *do* need to honor that whisper within that's pulling you toward something that aligns more with the life you want to live. Maybe that means carving out time for a passion outside of work, learning something new, or creating space for relationships that bring you joy.

You are brave enough to honor the call toward the life that feels like it was made for you. Trust that the voice inside, the one that knows what you truly want, is worth following, even when the path forward feels uncertain. You have what it takes to go after the life you want to live.

RECKLESSLY ALIVE AFFIRMATION

I AM BRAVE ENOUGH TO TAKE INTENTIONAL STEPS TOWARD A LIFE THAT FEELS TRUE.

REFLECTION

What's one area of your life where you've been ignoring that quiet inner voice? What is it trying to tell you about the life you truly want?

You can do this.

RECLAIM THE PERMISSION TO TRY

SIMPLE DOESN'T ALWAYS MEAN EASY, ESPECIALLY WHEN YOUR heart is in survival mode. Plans that seemed exciting when you made them can suddenly feel overwhelming when the time comes to follow through. Whether this means showing up for a friend, heading to the gym, or tackling a project that scares you, the temptation to retreat is real.

I've been there so many times, sitting in my car or pacing around my living room, convincing myself that I can't do it. The spiral of excuses starts: *What if I embarrass myself? What if it's too hard? What if I don't belong?* But I've learned to pause, take a breath, and tell myself something that's saved me more times than I can count: *I'll decide when I get there.*

There's freedom in giving yourself permission to try. You don't have to commit to seeing everything through yet. Simply take the first step. Head to the class. Walk into the event. Lace up your shoes. Tell yourself, *I'll go, and I'll decide when I get there.*

Nine times out of ten, once I'm out in the world, the negative spirals lose their grip. The gym feels less intimidating. The conversation I was dreading becomes a moment of connection. The thing I feared turns out to be far more manageable than

I thought. And if it doesn't? That's okay too. I can always step away, change my mind, or try again another day.

Reclaiming your power begins in your self-talk. The words you say to yourself shape how you move through fear. You don't have to feel confident or ready. You just need to speak to yourself with enough kindness to take the first step.

So today, give yourself permission to try. Let yourself go and see. Maybe the spiral will subside, or maybe it won't, but at least you'll know that you faced the moment instead of letting it slip away.

And each time you do that, you're showing your mind a new path forward, one quiet message, one brave step at a time. This is where it begins. This is what it sounds like when you tell yourself, *I can do this.*

RECKLESSLY ALIVE AFFIRMATION

I DON'T NEED TO HAVE ALL THE ANSWERS.
I AM CAPABLE OF MEETING THE MOMENT.

REFLECTION

What's one thing you've been avoiding because it feels too big or scary? How can you give yourself permission to try, knowing you can decide how to move forward once you're there?

You can do this.

DAY 38

RECLAIM YOUR AUTHENTICITY

WE'VE ALL HEARD THAT NAGGING VOICE—THE ONE URGING US TO be smaller, more reserved, or easier to digest. But let me ask you this: Has blending in ever made you feel alive? When I think back on my own life, the times I tried to shrink myself only left me feeling invisible, like a muted shadow of who I truly was. The lie we've been fed is that the world prefers a watered-down version of us. But the truth? The most magnetic thing about you is your authenticity.

Reclaiming your power starts with letting go of the need to be liked by everyone. You are not for everyone. And that's not just simply okay, it's also a gift. The right people won't be drawn to a diluted version of you. They'll lean in because of the bold dreams, unfiltered laughter, and interesting quirks that only you can bring. When you stop squeezing yourself into spaces never meant for you, you create room for people and opportunities that celebrate the real you.

Taking up space doesn't mean being loud for the sake of it. It's about standing firmly in your truth and saying, *This is who I am, and I deserve to be here*. Even when your voice wavers or your hands shake, choosing to show up authentically is a declaration of worth. And if someone decides you're "too much," let them go find less.

Reclaiming your authenticity is an act of love toward yourself.

It starts with rediscovering what lights you up: a long-forgotten hobby, a dream you've put on hold, or simply an appreciation for what makes you unique. It's setting boundaries that protect your energy and building relationships where you don't have to hide. Each time you honor your true self, you send a ripple into the world, a reminder that authenticity is a strength, not a flaw.

When you live unapologetically, you give others permission to do the same. Your courage becomes an invitation for others to stand in their truth. So let today be the day that you embrace all of who you are.

RECKLESSLY ALIVE AFFIRMATION

I AM WORTHY OF BEING SEEN AND HEARD.

REFLECTION

What part of yourself have you been hiding, and how can you begin to honor it? Where in your life can you unapologetically take up space?

You can do this.

RECLAIM PEACE IN THE PRESENT MOMENT

DURING MY HARDEST SEASONS, MY MIND FELT LIKE A STORM I couldn't calm. The past haunted me with memories of pain replaying on a loop until they felt like punishments I couldn't escape. I'd sit alone in my room, the air heavy and still, as those feelings washed over me. When I wasn't stuck in the past, I was lost in the future, catastrophizing every worst-case scenario until I felt paralyzed by fear.

Breaking free from that spiral wasn't easy; it rarely is. Sometimes it's like the gentle work of steering your thoughts back to the present, not fixing everything, just starting where you are.

For me, letting go of the past started with writing. I drafted letters to the people I needed to forgive, which I'd never send but that gave me space to process the weight I'd been carrying. I opened up to trusted friends and my therapist, whose perspectives helped me release the stories that had held me captive. And when the pain felt too big, simply stepping into the world, like sitting in a park and watching the world move, reminded me that I wasn't alone.

As for the future, I learned to meet my fears with a powerful mantra: *That's not today's problem*. I didn't need to plan five steps ahead; I just had to take one. Maybe that looked like sending a single message, opening the door and breathing in the air, or simply not hitting the snooze button. Those were small actions, but they mattered. We sometimes think resilience is found in grand gestures, but so often it begins in silence or in the tiniest decisions to keep going.

Reclaiming your power starts here in the small moments when you choose to move forward, even when it feels like everything inside you wants to give up. Each time you steady yourself and take the next step, you're rewriting what's possible.

Remind yourself: *The past is done. The future isn't here yet. My strength is in what I choose today.*

I still have tough days, but they no longer hold me captive, and one day, that will be your story too. Keep going, my friend. Healing and resilience are closer than they feel.

RECKLESSLY ALIVE AFFIRMATION

I AM HERE. I AM SAFE. I CAN HANDLE WHAT'S IN FRONT OF ME.

REFLECTION

Which thoughts tend to pull you away from the present? How can you redirect them? What small moments of peace can you create for yourself today?

You can do this.

DAY 40

RECLAIM YOUR LIFE WITH LITTLE ACTIONS

THE SINK WAS FULL AGAIN WITH WATER RIPPLING OVER A MESS OF forgotten dishes. I stood there staring, as if all the weight of my life had been dumped into that one small, insignificant task. Not because it mattered but because it felt like proof—proof that I was falling behind. Proof that I wasn't enough. And for the umpteenth day in a row, I made myself the same hollow promise: *I'll deal with it tomorrow.*

But tomorrow doesn't show up the way we think it will. Life doesn't transform in one glorious, cinematic moment of inspiration. The future we dream of is built here in the messy, ordinary now. Forget waiting for motivation or the stars to align. Change happens when we pick up the plate, close the drawer, or finally make that appointment.

Reclaiming your power doesn't come from some dramatic overhaul. It starts with one small action. A moment of defiance against the chaos. These tiny choices matter. They shift the story we tell ourselves. They take the narrative from *I can't keep up* to *I showed up anyway.*

The greatest act of self-care can be as simple as keeping a promise you made to yourself. Washing a single dish. Following through, even when it feels pointless. Not to prove anything to anyone else but to rebuild the trust that's been slowly worn thin between who you are and who you're trying to become.

If you're feeling overwhelmed by the weight of it all, I see you. I know how heavy life can feel and how impossible starting can seem. But start anyway, because it reminds you that you are always capable of creating momentum, one act of self-care and one dish at a time.

RECKLESSLY ALIVE AFFIRMATION

MY SELF-CARE IS A PRIORITY,
AND I AM WORTH THE EFFORT.

REFLECTION

What small action could you take today that feels grounding and meaningful? How can you bring intention into the time you already have?

You can do this.

DAY 41

RECLAIM YOUR POWER TO CHOOSE

IT'S NOT ALWAYS A DRAMATIC MOMENT WHEN YOU LOSE SIGHT OF yourself. Most of the time it happens gradually. You wake up one day, and the person in the mirror feels like a stranger—not because you made a huge mistake or took a wrong turn but because somewhere along the way, you stopped choosing for yourself.

Maybe it started small. You said yes to something you didn't want. You stayed silent when you should have spoken up. You took a step in a direction that didn't feel right, thinking it was temporary. And then another. And another. Until the path you were walking on was no longer your own.

Purpose isn't something you stumble across on some distant mountaintop. It's not a lightning strike or a perfect moment of clarity. Purpose is a practice, and it's one you reclaim every time you choose to live in alignment with the things that matter most to you.

Reclaiming your power starts when you ask yourself this: *When did I stop deciding? Where did I start shrinking?* It's noticing the places where you've handed over control—whether to fear, to obligation, or to someone else's expectations. It's realizing that power doesn't have to be earned or granted to you. It's been yours all along.

When I first started asking those questions, I didn't like the answers. I saw how much of my life I'd built around avoiding conflict, pleasing others, or simply surviving. But I also realized something freeing: I wasn't stuck. I didn't have to wait for anyone else to give me permission to change.

Reclaiming your power is less about searching and more about remembering. It's about returning to the things that light you up and deciding that those things are worth fighting for. It's turning back toward yourself, not in a self-centered way but in a way that says: *I am worth knowing. My voice is worth hearing. My life is worth living on my own terms.*

RECKLESSLY ALIVE AFFIRMATION

MY PURPOSE ISN'T SOMETHING I NEED TO FIND; IT'S SOMETHING I CAN CREATE, ONE INTENTIONAL STEP AT A TIME.

REFLECTION

Where in your life have you been following a path that doesn't feel like your own? What would it look like to take one step back toward yourself? What lights you up or makes you feel most alive, and how can you bring more of that into your daily choices?

You can do this.

RECLAIM YOURSELF IN RELATIONSHIPS

"WHAT'S YOUR FAVORITE ICE CREAM FLAVOR?" IT WASN'T A HARD question, but the silence that followed felt heavy. I had no answer. My mind raced, grasping for something definitive, something *mine*. Instead, I deflected with, "What's yours?"

It wasn't only ice cream. It was everything: my preferences, my voice, and my wants. I had somehow handed them over without even realizing it. For years, I'd bent and swayed to keep the peace, telling myself it didn't matter where we ate, what we watched, or what plans we made. Somewhere in the blur of being accommodating, I had let myself disappear.

Reclaiming your power isn't about being selfish or never compromising. It's about the quiet, steady work of remembering who you are. It's letting yourself ask, *What do I love? What lights me up?* And then it's answering, not for someone else's approval but for the simple joy of knowing your own heart again.

Start with small acts of defiance against the silence. Say, "Actually, I'm not in the mood for pizza." Or, "I drove to your place last time; do you mind coming this direction?" It was in these moments, when I said what I needed and let the chips fall where they may, that I started finding myself again.

And the most beautiful part? As I began to reclaim myself,

my relationships grew deeper. When you show up as your whole, authentic self, connection stops being about pleasing people and starts being about *knowing* them and letting them know you.

If you've lost your voice somewhere along the way, start here. Let yourself matter in the tiniest of ways. Choose something today—a meal, a song, a yes or no—that feels true to *you*. Because the people who love you don't want your silence. They want your presence, your truth, and your whole, unapologetic self.

RECKLESSLY ALIVE AFFIRMATION

MY NEEDS AND MY VOICE MATTER.

REFLECTION

What's one small choice you can make today to honor your voice? How might this bring you closer to yourself and those who care about you?

You can do this.

WEEK 7

CHANGING YOUR STORY

HAS YOUR LIFE EVER FELT LIKE A LOOP, EACH DAY A RERUN OF THE last? Like you're stuck on autopilot, just going through the motions? It's easy to believe that the story you're living is the only one you'll ever know. But here's the truth: You are the storyteller. The pen has always been in your hand, waiting for you to breathe something new onto the page.

This week is a chance to turn toward the unknown with curiosity and courage, to gently loosen the grip of old patterns and dare to imagine a narrative where you are free, alive, and deeply yourself. Each decision is a word, each bold step a sentence, each moment a chance to write a life that feels like home. The story isn't over; it's only beginning.

RECKLESSLY ALIVE WEEKLY CHALLENGE

Do something to spark joy and breathe more life into the ordinary. Lean in to a playful or silly moment that helps create a memory and makes life feel more enjoyable. Joy isn't a reward for getting everything right; it's a practice, and you deserve more of it.

LIVE A STORY WORTH TELLING

THE COLD WAS SHARP AND UNRELENTING, BITING THROUGH LAYers of clothing as if they weren't there. Snow stretched endlessly across the ground, and the wind roared through the trees with a force that felt alive. It was the second morning of our youth-group retreat, and I was soaking in the warmth of the lodge when the camp director's voice cut through the hum of breakfast chatter: "Polar Plunge at noon. Volunteers meet by the dining hall."

I shook my head before he'd even finished the announcement. No chance. It was 16 degrees outside, and they'd carved a hole in the ice so people could jump in. Who signs up for that? Apparently, Ethan, the seventh grader I mentored, had already decided that *we* did. "Sam, we have to do this!" His grin was wide and daring, like he knew exactly how to push my buttons.

"Absolutely not," I said, crossing my arms.

But Ethan wasn't buying it. "Come on. You're not scared, are you?"

That question landed like a dare, cracking open something I hadn't realized that I'd been carrying: fear. Not of the frigid water but of missing out. I'd spent so many years standing on the sidelines, letting doubt write my story. Not this time.

Later that day I stood at the edge of the ice, my breath visible in the freezing air. A crowd had gathered, their cheers rising into the sky as brave souls leaped into the black water. Ethan was grinning beside me, his excitement contagious. My heart raced as I stepped forward. The water was colder than I had imagined, a shock to every nerve. But as I surfaced, gasping and laughing, I felt something else—a sense of freedom, of life.

Changing your story doesn't mean rewriting your whole life in one day; it means choosing, moment by moment, to be the kind of person who creates memories worth holding on to. Because when you look back, it won't be the times you stayed comfortable that you remember. Each time you say yes to something that feels alive and true, you're rewriting the narrative of who you are and what you're capable of.

I hope you choose to do something today that makes you feel a little more brave. I hope you let yourself lean in to the discomfort enough to see what's on the other side. Because often, the things that feel the coldest and the scariest are the ones that leave you gasping, laughing, and feeling recklessly alive.

RECKLESSLY ALIVE AFFIRMATION

I HAVE THE POWER TO CHANGE MY STORY AND CREATE MOMENTS THAT MAKE ME FEEL ALIVE.

REFLECTION

When was the last time you did something that scared you? What's one way you could add a little more joy or adventure to your story this week?

You can do this.

DAY 44

CHANGE THE STORY YOU TELL YOURSELF

THE FITTING-ROOM LIGHTS WERE BRUTAL, BUZZING OVERHEAD, turning each mirror into a spotlight for everything I wished I couldn't see. The clothes on the bench looked more like a pile of failures. Each shirt and pair of pants seemed to shout the same thing: *You don't fit, and you never will.*

I wasn't just frustrated; I was exhausted from feeling like my body was the problem. Worn out from letting an industry convince me I wasn't enough because I didn't fit into some arbitrary mold. I yanked off the last shirt, tossed it aside, and stormed out of the fitting room, determined to be done: done with the day, done with shopping, done with feeling like a mistake.

That's when the woman at the try-on counter stopped me. She touched my arm gently and said eight words I'll never forget: "Baby, don't hate your body. Hate the clothes."

It wasn't only what she said but the permission in her voice, the reminder that the problem wasn't me. The problem was the story I'd been telling myself for years.

Changing your story starts in moments like these. The decision to challenge the voice in your head that says you're not enough. To realize that the world isn't always fair, and its standards aren't always kind, but you don't have to accept them as truth.

That day didn't magically change my self-talk. It did, however, crack something open. It reminded me that I don't have to live at war with myself.

The next time you hear that inner critic, pause. Ask yourself: *Is this thought helping me or hurting me? What is another perspective to the struggle I am having?* You have the power to change the narrative. The first step to rewriting your story is remembering that you're the one holding the pen.

RECKLESSLY ALIVE AFFIRMATION

I CHOOSE TO DESCRIBE MYSELF WITH WORDS
THAT HONOR MY STRENGTH AND GROWTH.

REFLECTION

What story have you been telling yourself about your worth? How can you start rewriting it into one that lifts you up?

You can do this.

DAY 45

PRACTICE LOVE IN MOTION

NEW YEAR'S EVE SHOULD'VE FELT LIGHT AND CELEBRATORY, glowing with the same gold flare as my cardboard party hat. But a heaviness kept tugging at me. I wasn't having the best day. My thoughts were scattered and my energy felt low, but I was trying. The table was full of laughter and clinking silverware, and candlelight flickered across half-empty glasses. I forced a smile, determined to stay present.

Then, partway through dinner, someone made a comment at my expense, the kind that's meant to be funny but slices deep anyway. Everyone laughed. I did, too, for half a second, until I felt my stomach drop and my mind start to spiral. My brain lit up like a panic alarm, and all I could think was, *I need to get out of here.*

That moment stayed with me, not because of what they said but because, for a second, I almost believed it. I almost let their words take hold of something tender in me, something I had spent years unlearning. That's the part no one sees—the inner battle after the laughter fades. The part where you must decide whether to keep carrying someone else's story or to offer yourself something kinder instead.

Loving yourself can feel like the most challenging thing, a quiet rebellion against the noise of everything you've ever been told you're not. It's layered and messy, tangled in the weight of old wounds and stories you've carried for too long. But let me remind you: If you're *trying* to love yourself, you already do.

Each time you choose a kinder word, each moment you resist the pull of self-judgment, every attempt to meet your reflection with gentleness; that's love in motion.

That night, I didn't stay at the table. I excused myself, stepped outside, and let the cold air hit my skin. I didn't tell myself to toughen up or get over it. I just took a few deep breaths and reminded myself, *I don't have to play along with old stories anymore.* The ones that say you're too sensitive. Too much. Not enough.

If you're trying to love yourself, you're doing it. Even when the old voices rise and you stumble, that effort is love in its truest form. Self-worth isn't a destination; it's the trying, the showing up, the grace you offer yourself in the middle of your mess. The effort you make, however small, is love in motion. You are worthy of that love—not someday but exactly as you are right now.

RECKLESSLY ALIVE AFFIRMATION

I CAN BE TENDER AND STRONG. I CAN FEEL HURT AND STILL KNOW THAT I'M WORTHY OF LOVE.

REFLECTION

What are the small, quiet ways you show up for yourself, even when it's hard? How can you see those acts as a reflection of your worth, not a reaction to doubt?

You can do this.

REFUSE TO BE SHAMED FOR YOUR STORY

THE DAY OF OUR THIRD DATE BEGAN WITH NERVOUS ANTICIPATION. I'd spent the morning trying to shake the excitement bubbling in my chest. My outfit felt right, I'd rehearsed casual conversation in my head, and the restaurant reservation was set. For a fleeting moment, I let myself believe that this could be something real. Then the message appeared on my screen, stealing all the air from the room: **I've thought more about it, and I don't think we're the right fit. I always saw myself marrying someone with a big, intact family.**

The words hit me harder than I expected. My chest tightened, and the questions followed. *Was it my fault that my dad left when I was twelve? Should I take the blame because my extended family didn't look like the kind you see in holiday commercials—the kind that stays close, shows up, and makes everything feel whole?* For years, I let people's comments like that shape how I saw myself, internalizing shame for circumstances that were never mine to control.

It's easy to let someone else's story about you become your truth. For years, I did. But changing your story begins with rewriting that narrative and refusing to carry a version of your story that was never yours to begin with. You can build the resilience it takes to refuse to let people shame you for circumstances out of your control.

I may not have a big, intact family, but I've built a chosen one—friends who show up, people who stay. The love I've created didn't come from tradition; it came from intention.

So no, that third date never happened. But something better did: I stopped letting someone else's judgment decide what my story could be. And if you've ever felt dismissed for something outside your control, know this: You're allowed to take the narrative back. You are the one who carries your full story, and you have the power to decide what it means from here.

RECKLESSLY ALIVE AFFIRMATION

I AM NO LONGER CARRYING SHAME FOR WHAT I DIDN'T CHOOSE.
I GET TO DEFINE WHAT MY STORY MEANS FROM HERE.

REFLECTION

What messages have others placed on your life that never truly belonged to you? How can you reclaim your story on your terms, with your voice?

You can do this.

DAY 47

CHANGE YOUR STORY BY TENDING TO YOUR ROOTS

OUTSIDE MY WINDOW, THE TREE BENDS WITH THE STORM. THE wind claws at its branches and the rain lashes its trunk, but it doesn't break. Each root clings to the earth with strength, unseen but unyielding. No matter how fierce the weather, the tree remains steady, alive, and growing.

Your life is like that tree. Self-care isn't about the leaves or the branches that everyone sees. It's about tending to your roots, the very foundation keeping you standing when life is too much. Those roots look different for everyone, but they often include rest, movement, connection, boundaries, and peace.

Some days, caring for your roots looks like an extra hour of sleep, a nourishing meal, or a walk outside with no destination in mind. Other days, it's letting yourself cry without explanation, staying home from an event you don't have the energy for, or texting a friend when you feel lonely. These choices matter. They may not be flashy, but they're powerful. They keep you standing.

When your body sighs, *I need rest,* honor it. When your mind pleads for space, give it room to breathe. When your heart aches for connection, reach out. When your spirit longs for some adventure, let it lead you.

Each decision to care for yourself, no matter how simple, is a declaration: *I am worth this. I am enough as I am.*

The storms may come, but when you nurture your roots, you'll find a steadiness within. The kind that allows you to weather whatever comes next. You'll stand tall, not because you're not shaken but because you've learned to anchor yourself in love and care.

RECKLESSLY ALIVE AFFIRMATION

WITH EVERY SMALL ACT OF SELF-CARE, I STRENGTHEN MY ROOTS AND CREATE A LIFE THAT FEELS GROUNDED AND TRUE.

REFLECTION

What's one way you can nourish and tend to the roots of your life today—physically, emotionally, mentally, or spiritually?

You can do this.

THE STORY IS STILL UNFOLDING

THE WORLD WHISPERS THAT TIME IS RUNNING OUT, THAT THE years slip away like sand through our fingers. With every passing birthday, we're told that we're nearing the end of something—of youth, of opportunity, of purpose. But what if that's all simply noise?

Purpose isn't chained to a calendar. It doesn't care how many years have passed, how many things you've yet to do, or how far you've veered from the path you had imagined for yourself. It's always there, quietly waiting for you to show up. Like an old friend whose hand you're meant to hold, no matter how many seasons have passed.

There was a time in my life when every unchecked box felt like failure, as if the clock were running out and I was falling behind. But as the years have piled up, I've come to see something different: Age isn't the end of anything; it's the beginning of deeper wisdom, richer experiences, and knowing yourself in ways you never could have when you were younger.

Changing your story doesn't require rewriting the past; it starts by claiming who you are right now and choosing what comes next. You're not bound by age, or what you thought was possible, or the timeline others have set. Each new chapter of life, no matter how far along in the book you are, holds the potential for a fresh start, a new direction, and a deeper meaning.

You're not too old. It's not too late. You can still dream. You can still feel the fire that once burned within you, even if it's been buried under years of doubt, disappointments, or what others said you couldn't do. Purpose doesn't die out; it evolves, and with it, so do you. Your purpose is not bound by time; it's alive and waiting for you to live it.

RECKLESSLY ALIVE AFFIRMATION

I AM NOT BOUND BY TIMELINES OR DEADLINES.
MY PURPOSE MOVES WITH ME.

REFLECTION

What's one pull or whisper you've been ignoring in your life, or that seems like it has died out? What would it feel like to revive it today?

You can do this.

DAY 49

WHEN OLD STORIES DON'T FIT ANYMORE

LAUGHTER FILLED THE AIR, BRIGHT AND WARM, THE KIND THAT feels like coming home. After spending a few years apart, I'd decided to reconnect with an old group of friends. That first hangout was pure magic. We swapped stories and resurrected inside jokes I'd forgotten, and for a moment it felt like no time had passed.

But as we started meeting up more often, something began to shift. I'd leave each gathering feeling hollow, like I was carrying a deep sadness I hadn't arrived with. When I got home, I wanted to crawl under the covers and disappear for a few days. My instinct was to pull away, but instead, I decided to go one more time and stay curious about what was causing this emotional shift.

The next time we got together, the truth hit me: I was slipping back into an old version of myself that I'd worked so hard to outgrow. The familiar patterns were there, clear as day. I was the butt of every joke, my voice was drowned out, and I found myself shrinking with every laugh at my expense.

It wasn't only their fault. They were falling back into the roles we'd always played because that's who I *used to be*. I used to let people walk all over me. I didn't speak up, didn't believe that I deserved better, and didn't think I could ask for more.

The years apart had changed me. I'd spent those years doing the hard, messy work of becoming someone I could be proud of who sets boundaries, protects their peace, and refuses to shrink to fit in. And now there was this tension between who I'd been and who I was becoming.

Not everyone will grow with you when you do the hard work of changing your story. I hope you allow them to meet the new you and readjust to the new dynamic. And if they don't, I hope you let them go with peace and grace, knowing that your growth is worth protecting.

It's uncomfortable to realize that the spaces you used to fit in now feel suffocating. The people who genuinely love you will celebrate the person you're becoming, not try to pull you back into the past. Your growth deserves space to flourish, and you deserve relationships that help you show up as your best self and embrace the peaceful future you're fighting for.

RECKLESSLY ALIVE AFFIRMATION

I DESERVE RELATIONSHIPS THAT SUPPORT WHO I AM BECOMING.

REFLECTION

Where in your life are you shrinking to fit into old relationships? How can you create space for people who embrace the person you're becoming?

You can do this.

WEEK 8

GROUNDED IN GRATITUDE

GRATITUDE ROOTS US IN WHAT'S STEADY AND TRUE. IT DOESN'T erase the hard seasons or make challenges disappear, but it shifts how we carry them. Gratitude is more than a list of things we're thankful for; it's a grounding practice, a lens that helps us see the world through clarity and hope. It anchors us in the present moment, reminding us of the good that exists alongside the struggle.

This week, we'll explore how gratitude can ground us: finding it amid difficulty, sharing it with others, and weaving it into our everyday lives. Gratitude transforms our outlook and strengthens our foundations, and it offers a steady place to grow, heal, and step into who we're becoming.

RECKLESSLY ALIVE WEEKLY CHALLENGE

This week, choose a way to practice gratitude. Each day, write down three things you're thankful for. Tell someone how they've impacted your life. Or take a moment to appreciate something simple like a sunrise, a meal, a moment of peace. Let gratitude ground you in the present and remind you of what truly matters.

DON'T LEAVE GRATITUDE UNSPOKEN

HIGH SCHOOL FELT LIKE A NIGHTMARE I COULDN'T ESCAPE: SLAMming locker doors, whispered rumors, and the ache of never quite fitting in. But the moment I stepped into that room, the world softened. The hum of piano keys filled the air, blending with voices that carried more than music; they carried hope.

She was the kind of teacher who saw you, not only your grades or your potential but the person inside. "Your voice matters," she'd say, and for that hour, I almost believed her. For one precious slice of my day, I felt like I belonged and didn't have to prove or pretend.

Years later, I went back. I stood in that same room, a little older, a little braver, and told her what I hadn't been able to say before: "Thank you. You saved me in ways you'll never know." She smiled her usual smile, kind and unassuming, and waved it off with a quick, "Oh, please. That's what teachers do." But I saw how her eyes softened.

We don't talk enough about how terrifying it can be to speak gratitude into the world. It's easy to assume that people already know how much they mean to us. But even if they know, they need to hear it. A heartfelt thank-you is one of the best ways to repay someone for the love they've shown us. It doesn't have to be polished but should be real. And yes, your voice might crack, or you might stumble over your words, but that's okay. What matters is that you say them.

Being grounded in gratitude invites us to pause and notice the people, moments, and lessons that have shaped us. It becomes something more than a feeling; it becomes a way of moving through the world with intention. Gratitude doesn't just soften your heart but also moves your feet, opens your mouth, and changes the course of a relationship with a few honest words.

RECKLESSLY ALIVE AFFIRMATION

I CHOOSE TO SHARE MY GRATITUDE BOLDLY, KNOWING THAT MY WORDS HAVE THE POWER TO HEAL AND CONNECT.

REFLECTION

Who's someone you've been meaning to thank but haven't yet? What's one way you can send gratitude out into the world for that person this week?

You can do this.

THE GRATITUDE YOU OWE YOURSELF

THE DAY I FINALLY PAUSED TO THANK MYSELF DIDN'T SEEM remarkable. I was sitting in my car after a long, exhausting afternoon, staring at the glow of a fast-food sign through my windshield. My to-do list was only half finished, and my brain was replaying every awkward moment of the day like a broken record. I sighed, gripped the steering wheel, then for some reason whispered, "Thank you."

It wasn't planned. It slipped out. "Thank you for trying. Thank you for showing up, even when you didn't feel like it." The words felt strange, even ridiculous, but the tightness in my chest eased a little. I sat there, headlights reflecting off the wet pavement, and realized how long it had been since I'd given myself credit for simply making it through.

Lots of people talk about the importance of showing gratitude to others, and yes, it matters. Thank the friend who shows up, the coworker who helps out, the stranger who holds the door. But when's the last time you thanked yourself—the one who gets you out of bed each morning, pushes through the hard days, and still holds on to hope? What would it feel like to stop and say, "Thank you for getting me here"?

Being grounded in gratitude means noticing not just what's

good around you but also the strength it's taken to get here. It includes the big wins, yes, but also the quiet moments—the days you showed up when you felt empty and the times you held on when everything in you wanted to let go.

Thanking yourself doesn't have to be a big production. Maybe it's as simple as whispering, "Thank you for making it through" or pausing for a moment while brushing your teeth to think, *Even if it wasn't perfect, I'm proud of my effort today.* Gratitude, the real kind, doesn't wait for everything to be perfect. It begins with noticing what's already there.

So tonight, when the world is still and you're alone with your thoughts, try it. Say the words you've been waiting to hear. "Thank you for trying. Thank you for staying. Thank you for being here."

RECKLESSLY ALIVE AFFIRMATION

I AM PROUD OF MY EFFORT, NO MATTER HOW SMALL.

REFLECTION

How can you begin to acknowledge the strength within you, even on days when you don't feel your best? What's one thing you can thank yourself for this week?

You can do this.

DAY 52

GRATITUDE IN THE INSECURITIES

SITTING AT A COFFEE SHOP WITH A DEAR FRIEND, THE WARMTH OF my cup did little to calm the cold knot of insecurity tightening in my chest. The whir of the café blender faded into the background as my thoughts swirled, caught in a quiet storm. I paused, hands trembling, and said, "Can I speak an insecurity? Do you feel like I'm talking about myself too much? I worry about that and don't mean to take over the conversation."

Her eyes softened as she laughed gently, saying, "Oh my gosh, not at all. I asked about it!" Later, she added, "You taught me something today: I can speak my insecurities too."

That moment stayed with me, not because it erased my self-doubt but because I didn't let fear decide how honest I could be. I spoke the hard thing and stayed. And afterward, something surprising showed up: gratitude. Not the shiny, performative kind but something deeper. Gratitude for how far I've come. For the kind of connection that honesty makes possible. For the small, brave voice in me that said it out loud.

I used to think self-worth came from feeling confident all the time. Now I'm learning that it looks more like staying with myself, even when doubt creeps in. Gratitude feels connected to that, like an acknowledgment of effort, of presence. When I can recognize the moments when I've chosen honesty instead of silence, something in me softens. I start to feel proud of the way I've kept showing up, even when it was hard.

If you've been holding something inside, such as an insecurity you've been afraid to name, maybe this is your reminder that it's okay to speak it. You don't need to be perfect to be honest. You don't have to wait until the fear is gone to say what's true. Each time you let yourself be real, you're building something stronger within yourself. And when you do, let gratitude meet you there. Let it remind you that your effort matters. Your voice matters. And the version of you who shows up, even with shaking hands, is already enough.

RECKLESSLY ALIVE AFFIRMATION

I AM WORTHY OF LOVE AND CONNECTION,
EXACTLY AS I AM, FLAWS AND ALL.

REFLECTION

How can you express your insecurities today, grounding yourself in gratitude for who you are in this moment?

You can do this.

DAY 53

CHOOSE GRATITUDE WHEN IT'S HARD

THE WORRIES WEREN'T ONLY IN MY MIND; THEY LINGERED IN MY body, creating a heaviness that made even small tasks feel impossible. I remember sitting at my kitchen table one gray afternoon, the light outside dull and uninviting. I'd been trying to force myself to work, to be productive, and to "snap out of it," but the weight wouldn't lift. My thoughts looped endlessly with regrets from years ago, fears about the future, things I hadn't said, choices I couldn't undo. It felt like my mind was closed off to hope, as if it had sealed the doors and drawn the curtains just in case anything bright tried to slip in. Even when I longed to feel thankful, gratitude felt unreachable, like trying to grasp something I'd never truly known.

There are days when resilience comes down to choosing to find one small thing that doesn't hurt. Gratitude won't sweep in to fix your problems or erase your pain, but it can remind you of the goodness around you. A stranger's smile. The warmth of a fresh cup of tea. The familiar melody of a song that once made you feel like yourself.

Gratitude can live alongside pain. It can sit with you in the discomfort and still help you notice what hasn't disappeared. It's the act of saying *thank you*—not because everything is perfect but because you've chosen to stay open to what's still good (even when your brain doesn't want to see it).

Gratitude doesn't diminish the weight of your challenges, but it can offer perspective. Nothing may have changed externally, but that small shift in awareness can change how you carry what hurts. Light and shadow don't cancel each other out; they coexist. And when hope feels distant, noticing even one gentle thing can be the most resilient act of all.

Even when life feels heavy, gratitude gently whispers, "You're still here. Keep looking. There's more to this story than the hard parts."

RECKLESSLY ALIVE AFFIRMATION

GRATITUDE IS MY STRENGTH. I CHOOSE TO NOTICE THE LIGHT, EVEN WHEN SHADOWS LINGER.

REFLECTION

What's one small moment of beauty or comfort you can hold on to today? How can gratitude remind you of one good thing, even in the mess?

You can do this.

DAY 54

GRATITUDE FOR THE QUIET MIRACLES

STEAM CURLED FROM THE MUG BETWEEN MY HANDS AS I LEANED against the kitchen counter, the late-afternoon sun casting long shadows across the floor. Music played low from my record player, the first time in months I'd had the energy to select an album off the shelf. I wasn't trying to fix anything or outrun a thought. I was just . . . standing there. Breathing. And somehow, that unexpected stillness felt like a victory.

I've lived through times where every step felt like a battle, where even the simplest acts of care seemed impossible. And yet, when life became easier, I forgot to whisper "thank you." Isn't that the paradox of healing? We spend so long clawing toward steady ground that we almost fail to see it when it arrives.

Lately, I've been paying attention to the tiny shifts: rinsing dishes right after I eat instead of letting them pile up. Choosing a meal that actually sounds good instead of just whatever's quickest. Laughing, *really* laughing, at a TV show without checking out halfway through. These aren't dramatic changes. No one else would see them as milestones. But I do.

When I notice them, I try to say thank you. These small moments, the ones I used to rush through or avoid, start to feel like glimpses of something lighter, something steadier and a little more alive.

So if you're in a season where self-care feels like a struggle, start by noticing what's already shifting. Maybe you took a break so you wouldn't burn out. Maybe you finally scheduled the appointment you've been putting off. Maybe you showed yourself patience in a moment that used to end in shame. You don't need a perfect routine in order to find healing. Sometimes it's the thank-you for what's working that helps you keep going. Gratitude reminds you that even small acts of self-care are real care, and that's more than enough for today.

RECKLESSLY ALIVE AFFIRMATION

I WILL NOTICE THE SMALL WAYS I'M ALREADY CARING FOR MYSELF AND LET THAT BE ENOUGH.

REFLECTION

What signs of progress have you overlooked in your daily routine? How can you practice gratitude for the care you're already giving yourself?

You can do this.

GRATITUDE IN ACTION

THE PUERTO RICAN SUN WAS RELENTLESS AS WE EXITED THE VAN in Juana Díaz. The air felt thick, carrying the weight of heat and loss. Before us stood Luis, a man whose home had been reduced to fragments—crumbling walls and a roof patched with a blue tarp. His little boy clung to his hand, and his wife stood nearby, their smiles unwavering despite all they had endured.

We labored for a week for this family. Our hands grew blistered and our clothes were streaked with dust, but every task felt sacred. At lunch we gathered in the backyard, sharing sandwiches and listening to Luis. Through a translator, he told us about the storm, the chaos, the long year they'd spent under that fragile tarp, and how he still woke up grateful each day.

As we drove away that final afternoon, I watched Luis standing in front of his newly repaired house with his arm wrapped around his wife's shoulder. Their little boy giggled, racing barefoot across the porch we had built. And in that moment, I understood something I hadn't before: Gratitude doesn't just acknowledge what we've been given; it multiplies it.

When we let gratitude guide our actions, it becomes a force for connection, healing, and restoration. Feeling thankful is only the beginning; the real blessing is living in a way that reflects it.

Purpose rarely shouts. You might find it in the work of showing up with your whole heart, hammering one nail at a time. Or it might be in the stillness, offering what you can, listening closely, and staying present. Some days, it could just be sitting on a porch in the fading light, realizing that even this can be holy. If you're feeling lost or unsure of your next step, start with gratitude. Let it remind you, like Luis reminded me, of the strength you carry, the goodness still within reach, and the difference you're capable of making. Some days the clearest direction comes when you offer what you have to someone else. And when you do, don't be surprised if the act of lifting others lifts something in you too.

RECKLESSLY ALIVE AFFIRMATION

I AM GRATEFUL FOR THE OPPORTUNITIES TO GIVE, KNOWING THAT PURPOSE IS BUILT THROUGH SMALL, INTENTIONAL ACTS OF CARE.

REFLECTION

How can gratitude guide your actions this week? What's one small way you can use what you have in order to make a difference for someone else?

You can do this.

GRATITUDE IN OUR SHARED HUMANITY

THE WEDDING WAS BEAUTIFUL—EVERY DETAIL PERFECT, EVERY laugh polished. But as I stood there, surrounded by the glow of fairy lights and swirling conversations, I felt more invisible than I had in years. The small talk felt like static, and the questions about my love life—"Are you even trying to date?"—sliced like little paper cuts. I slipped out early, the ache in my chest growing heavier with every step.

The city streets were still, and the cold bit my cheeks. That's when I saw him: a man with a red beard slumped on a bench, his cigarette glowing faintly. He didn't look up, but something urged me to say hi.

"Hey," I said, walking over. His eyes flickered up, cautious but kind. "How's it going?"

His name was Bill, and soon, the story of his life spilled out: homelessness, ADHD, years of struggle. But his voice carried something more than pain. He told me about his twelve days of sobriety, his pride palpable. I felt a shift as we sat together, drinking coffee and sharing stories. He was resilient, open, human.

As the night wound down, I opened up to him too. I told him about my recent heartbreak and this lonely evening. He leaned back on the bench, eyes steady. "Well, anyone would be lucky to be with you," he said, quiet but firm. "You're cool as hell."

His words startled me, not because they were extraordinary but because they were exactly what I needed to hear. I'd walked into that exchange with Bill thinking I was the one giving—time, coffee, connection. But he gave just as much, and I was overcome with gratitude for him. He reminded me that showing up for someone else doesn't only help them; it helps you too.

Being grounded in gratitude involves recognizing that connection is a two-way street. It's in those shared moments, the give-and-take, that we find purpose. Bill and I didn't fix each other that night, but we reminded each other of what it feels like to be seen and to matter.

So if you're in the middle of something that feels uncertain or vulnerable, keep going. You don't have to be perfect to make a difference; you just need to stay open. Connection might find you exactly where you are. And when it does, don't be surprised if you're just as changed by what you receive as by what you give.

RECKLESSLY ALIVE AFFIRMATION

EVERY PERSON I MEET HAS SOMETHING TO TEACH ME.

REFLECTION

Who has shown up for you in ways you didn't expect? How can you offer that same gift to someone today?

You can do this.

WEEK 9

TRUSTING THE PROCESS

THE BEGINNING OF CHANGE FEELS ELECTRIC—NEW HABITS, fresh possibilities, the spark of something better within reach. But as the days stretch on, that initial shine starts to dim. Progress feels slow, and doubt creeps in: *I'm not moving fast enough. I'm slipping back. This will never work.* When results aren't immediate, it's easy to let those thoughts take hold.

But transformation doesn't follow a quick or flashy timeline. Growth is steady and quiet, unfolding beneath the surface where it's not always visible. Each choice to keep going, every step forward when giving up feels easier, is building something real and lasting. Trust that your effort today is creating the strength you'll lean on tomorrow.

RECKLESSLY ALIVE WEEKLY CHALLENGE

Make time for a hobby that brings you joy or try something new just for the fun of it. Learn a few phrases in a new language, cook a recipe you've never tried, or explore a creative outlet without feeling pressure. You're allowed to do things simply because they light you up.

TRUST THE CRINGE

WHEN I STARTED MY WRITING CAREER, IT DIDN'T LOOK LIKE MUCH of a career at all. It began with a blog: just me, my thoughts, and a few posts I wasn't even sure anyone would read. One day, while standing in a group at church, I overheard someone say, "Why does everyone think we care what they have to say? Have you read his blog? It's so embarrassing."

I froze. The words hit me like a slap, sharp and unfiltered in the noisy room. They weren't talking about just *any* blog; they were talking about *mine*. And they didn't even realize that I was standing right there. My face flushed as I tried to swallow the knot rising in my throat.

It wasn't the last time someone mocked me or questioned why I was putting myself out there. People rolled their eyes at my posts for years and whispered their judgment behind my back. And honestly? I wondered if they were right.

But something inside me refused to stop. There was a deep and unrelenting pull to create, share my story, and put words into the world in the hope that they might mean something to someone.

Trusting the process of starting something new doesn't always feel empowering. Often, it feels awkward, vulnerable, or downright painful. But taking bold action—like signing up for a night class when you haven't studied in years, performing at your first open mic, telling someone how you actually feel, sharing an idea in a meeting when you're the youngest in the room, or showing up to a community event where you don't know anyone—is where transformation begins.

Even when your hands tremble and the voices of doubt grow loud, keep going, my friend. Every cringe-worthy start, every moment of self-doubt, every shaky first step is proof that you are in motion. You're building something that matters.

Years later, that same guy who called my blog embarrassing sent me a message. He was launching a music project and wondered if I'd promote it to my social media audience. I laughed when I saw it, not out of spite but because it reminded me of how far I'd come, cringe and all.

One day, those who doubted you, and maybe even the version of you that doubted yourself, will see what was true all along: You were building something meaningful, one brave step at a time.

RECKLESSLY ALIVE AFFIRMATION

I AM BUILDING SOMETHING EXTRAORDINARY,
ONE BOLD STEP AT A TIME.

REFLECTION

What's something you've wanted to try or create but haven't because you're afraid it might feel awkward or messy? What would it look like to give yourself permission to do it anyway?

You can do this.

DAY 58

SAY IT ANYWAY

I LEANED ON THE BATHROOM COUNTER AS I WIPED AWAY THE FOG, staring at the tired face looking back at me. My hair was a mess, my eyes were still puffy from a rough night of sleep, and my inner critic was already revving up. *I look awful. I'm falling behind. Why even try today?*

I hesitated, toothbrush in hand, then muttered under my breath, "You look nice today."

It felt ridiculous. Like I was playacting in a scene I didn't believe. But I said it again, louder this time. "You look nice today."

And for a split second, something shifted. The voice in my head didn't magically change, but I had interrupted it. I had chosen a new script—one that, even if it felt awkward, was rooted in care rather than criticism.

Changing the way we speak to ourselves can feel unnatural, even embarrassing. It's so much easier to default to what we've always heard or believed. But self-talk is a practice. A process. A tiny act of rebellion against the stories that try to keep us small.

And it's in the choices we make. Saying, "I'm proud of you," when the day doesn't go as planned. Saying, "You're doing enough," when the to-do list still has twenty things on it. Saying, "You're still worthy," when the mirror doesn't reflect the version of you that the world seems to value.

None of this will feel easy at first. It might sound fake or forced, but speak it anyway. Because the more you say it, the more your brain learns it. And over time, those kind words stop sounding so foreign, and they start sounding like you.

So when that old voice shows up and tries to pull you into the spiral of shame or self-doubt, pause and offer something gentler. Speak to yourself like someone who deserves love and patience—because you do.

This is how change begins. I know because I've been exactly where you are, relearning how to speak to myself one kind word at a time, one moment at a time where I chose to build myself up rather than tear myself down. That voice you're practicing is shaping how you'll show up for everything that comes next.

Even if you don't fully believe it yet, trust the process and say it anyway.

RECKLESSLY ALIVE AFFIRMATION

MY WORDS HAVE POWER, AND I CHOOSE TO SPEAK TO MYSELF WITH KINDNESS.

REFLECTION

What's one phrase you can start saying to yourself, either out loud or in your mind, that feels kind and true, even if part of you isn't sure you believe it yet?

You can do this.

TRUST YOU'RE ENOUGH AS YOU ARE

FOR YEARS, I THOUGHT HAPPINESS WAS WAITING BEYOND THE next achievement. I chased milestones like they were golden keys to finally unlocking the version of myself I'd be proud of. A new job, a relationship, a big win—each felt like the answer. And yet, even when I crossed the finish line, the doubts were still there, stubborn as ever. The glow always faded faster than I'd hoped, leaving me with the same question: *Why don't I feel any different?*

No accomplishment or external marker will ever fill the space meant for self-acceptance. If you don't believe you're enough without the goal, you won't believe it once you get there either. The validation you're searching for must come from within, not from what you do or have.

So how do you decide to be enough? How do you shift the story you've told yourself for so long? Here are a few ideas:

- **Rewrite the script.** When you hear that inner voice saying, *I'm not enough*, remind yourself that you don't need a new achievement to be worthy, and say, "I'm doing my best, and that's enough for today."
- **Celebrate what is.** Stop waiting for the next milestone to feel good enough. Instead, recognize the wins you've

already had, big or small, and appreciate where you are right now.

- **Practice self-compassion.** When you stumble, don't let it reinforce the idea that you're not enough. Embrace failure as a way of learning and treat yourself with the kindness you deserve.

Trusting the process of progress means choosing to believe that you are enough, right here, right now—not in some far-off future or when your life looks a certain way, but today, right here in this messy, complicated, and beautiful moment.

You are enough without your finish line, whatever that looks like for you. And when you trust that thought, the journey becomes the reward.

RECKLESSLY ALIVE AFFIRMATION

I AM WORTHY TODAY, NOT BECAUSE OF WHAT I'VE ACHIEVED BUT BECAUSE OF WHO I AM.

REFLECTION

What's one area of your life where you've been waiting to feel like you're "enough"? How can you remind yourself that you already are?

You can do this.

TRUST THE QUIET PROGRESS

IT'S JANUARY AND THE GYM IS PACKED WITH TREADMILLS BUZZing, weights clanking, and water bottles thudding on rubber floors. There's a collective energy in the air, a silent agreement to try. Try to be stronger. Try to be consistent. Try to change something. But by February, the crowd thins. The momentum slips. One skipped workout turns into two, and soon, the voice of doubt sneaks in: *What's the point?*

Somewhere along the way, we started believing that progress counts only if it's flawless. That if we break the streak or miss a step, it's over. But the process of becoming, healing, building, and becoming more fully yourself was never meant to be pristine. It's meant to be lived in, stretched, revisited, and sometimes, restarted.

Maybe your goal had nothing to do with fitness. Maybe it was reading more before bed instead of scrolling. Eating more meals at home. Drinking water in the morning. Saving money. Putting yourself out there more. And maybe you started strong until life got complicated. That doesn't make you a failure; it makes you human.

What matters is your choice to keep going. Let today be about what you *can* do, not what you *didn't* do.

Resilience shows up in the decision to try again. Not just once but again and again, even when you feel off track or when no one else sees how hard you're working to stay in it. That quiet persistence is something to be proud of.

So take a breath. Regroup. Begin again. You haven't lost your progress; you're just in the middle of the process. And that's exactly where the transformation is happening.

You can do this, my friend. Trust the quiet progress and don't give up.

RECKLESSLY ALIVE AFFIRMATION

I AM NOT DEFINED BY MY SETBACKS.
EACH DAY IS A CHANCE TO TRUST MY
JOURNEY AND HONOR MY PROGRESS.

REFLECTION

How can you release guilt for what hasn't gone perfectly? How can you refocus on what's possible today?

You can do this.

DAY 61

TRUST CURIOSITY OVER JUDGMENT

THE TRAIL WAS DAMP FROM LAST NIGHT'S RAIN, THE AIR COOL and earthy as I ran beneath a canopy of pine. My feet moved instinctively, dodging roots and sinking slightly into soft soil. I hadn't set out to find peace; I just needed to get out of my head. But somewhere between breaths, the noise began to fade. I didn't feel calm in the traditional sense, but I felt *okay*. I felt like myself again.

That's the thing about self-care: It doesn't always look the way you're told it should. For years, I tried to mold myself into other people's versions of tranquility: perfectly lit journaling corners, singing sound bowls, soothing meditation apps. But every time, I felt like I was pretending. The stillness didn't settle me. The routines didn't stick. And I started to wonder if maybe I was just bad at self-care.

Turns out, there was nothing wrong with me. I just hadn't found what worked *for me* yet. When I stopped judging myself, however, something shifted. I began to ask softer questions: *What might help me instead? What feels rejuvenating to me?*

Maybe calm lives in the ritual of fixing something with your hands, or in the weight of a book that keeps you turning pages late into the night. Maybe stillness shows up while deep cleaning, or tossing a ball with your dog at dusk, or standing in the aisle of a hardware store with nowhere else to be. Maybe what soothes you isn't soft lighting and whispered mantras but loud music and a long drive, or organizing your garage until the world feels a little more in order. Maybe peace looks like lighting a firepit just because, or getting lost in a spreadsheet that makes your mind feel clear again. Maybe self-care for you isn't still at all. Maybe it's movement, tinkering, building, breathing.

The journey to self-care is deeply personal, and learning to trust it means honoring your own rhythm—one that's messy, beautiful, and uniquely yours. So stay curious. Keep experimenting. You're not failing if it looks different than someone else's version. You're learning how to care for yourself in the way you need most. That alone is brave. That alone is enough.

RECKLESSLY ALIVE AFFIRMATION

I HONOR MY JOURNEY BY STAYING CURIOUS
ABOUT WHAT RESTORES ME.

REFLECTION

What's one way you've judged yourself for not fitting into a traditional self-care mold? How can you explore self-care practices that align with who you are, not who you think you should be?

You can do this.

DAY 62

JOY AT REGISTER SIX

I WAS HAVING A ROUGH DAY, THE KIND WHERE EVERYTHING FEELS like too much and your brain won't stop buzzing. Not a meltdown, just heavy. I needed a few groceries, so I headed to the store down the street, hoping the errand might help reset something for me.

The checkout line was long, as always, but not because it was slow; it was because everyone wanted to be in *her* line. She wore big, colorful earrings that swung when she moved and sparkly acrylic nails that changed designs each week. Her perfume hit you three customers deep, and somehow this was comforting. She greeted everyone like an old friend.

She spotted me and lit up. "Hey there, Sam! How's your mom doing?"

Her energy was electric—dancing behind the counter, cracking jokes with the guy ahead of me, complimenting a little girl's light-up shoes. And somehow, just by being herself, she turned my day around. I left that store feeling lighter than when I had walked in.

Not everyone sees working a grocery store register as a place of purpose. I heard a high school teacher once say, "Study hard, or you'll end up working in retail your whole life," like that was the worst-case scenario. But he obviously had never met *her*. Now that I'm older, I can see it clearly: That cashier is living with more joy, more purpose, and more impact than that grumpy math teacher ever did.

And maybe that's what trusting the process really looks like: not chasing some close-minded idea of success but pouring your energy into what's right in front of you: turning ordinary moments into connection. Making people feel seen, even in the most overlooked corners of the world.

So wherever life finds you, I hope you choose to be a little more like my local cashier—showing up fully, offering a smile when no one expects it, learning someone's name, turning a checkout line into a place people actually want to be. Because the most meaningful kind of purpose isn't found in a title or destination. It's in how you show up, with joy, generosity, and love, right where you are.

RECKLESSLY ALIVE AFFIRMATION

I DON'T NEED A TITLE OR A PLAN TO HAVE PURPOSE.
THE WAY I SHOW UP CAN BE MEANINGFUL, JUST AS I AM.

REFLECTION

Where in your daily life do you have the chance to bring light, connection, or joy to someone else—even in small ways?

You can do this.

DAY 63

TRUST THE PROCESS OF FRIENDSHIP

MY FIRST DAY OF COLLEGE WORK-STUDY IN THE CAFETERIA WASN'T exactly the start of anything extraordinary. I was assigned to the bakery with a girl named Emily, and both of us were shy and wary of what we had gotten ourselves into. The instructions were simple: "Take the freight elevator down to the lowest level," the manager had said, handing us trays of dough. "Put this on the racks, mop the floors, and grab a soda until your shift ends." The air downstairs felt cool and held an odor, like sugar mixed with industrial floor cleaner, that clung to your clothes by the end of the shift.

Emily and I worked in silence at first, keeping to our own thoughts as we navigated unfamiliar tasks. We had wondered how we ended up here, each unsure of the other. But over time, conversation trickled in—small comments about the dough, laughs about how the mop handle kept sticking, and eventually, questions about classes, dorm life, and what was to come.

Looking back, it's remarkable how our paths continued to overlap. A few years later, we were paired for our first teaching assignments. Her dorm room was above mine senior year, and we crossed paths most mornings. Life kept us close even after college; our first teaching jobs landed us only thirty miles apart in rural Iowa. Though life changed, the connection stayed.

Emily isn't the friend I would've predicted I'd keep for life, but she's one I'm beyond grateful for. Through moves, new jobs, and heartbreaks, she's shown up with kindness, encouragement, and unwavering support.

Trusting the process of connection means letting relationships take shape without trying to force them. People come into our lives for a reason, a season, or a lifetime, and we don't always know which one it will be at the start. Relationships grow best when they're given space to unfold at their own pace, without pressure for instant depth or certainty. All we can do is stay open to timing we don't control, to people we don't expect, and to a bigger plan we may not recognize while riding a freight elevator with a stranger who might become family.

We may not always know who will witness the width of our story, and we don't need to. We just need to keep making room for the ones who feel like sunlight, especially in the basement.

RECKLESSLY ALIVE AFFIRMATION

I TRUST THAT THE CONNECTIONS MEANT FOR
ME WILL DEVELOP AT THEIR OWN PACE.

REFLECTION

Who in your life has surprised you by becoming important? How can you nurture that connection today?

You can do this.

WEEK 10

HEARING FROM YOUR FUTURE SELF

WHAT IF YOU COULD HEAR FROM THE PERSON YOU'RE BECOMING? What might they gently reflect upon about this chapter of your life? Maybe they'd remind you of the strength you've forgotten or help you see the beauty hidden in the moments you often overlook. This week is an invitation to imagine the wisdom, encouragement, and kindness your future self might whisper back into today—to step outside your current perspective and view your life through eyes shaped by time, growth, and grace.

As you move through these days, carry that voice with you—the one that knows how far you've come and how much is still possible. Let it guide you with quiet courage, knowing that the choices you make now are already shaping a story you'll be proud to tell.

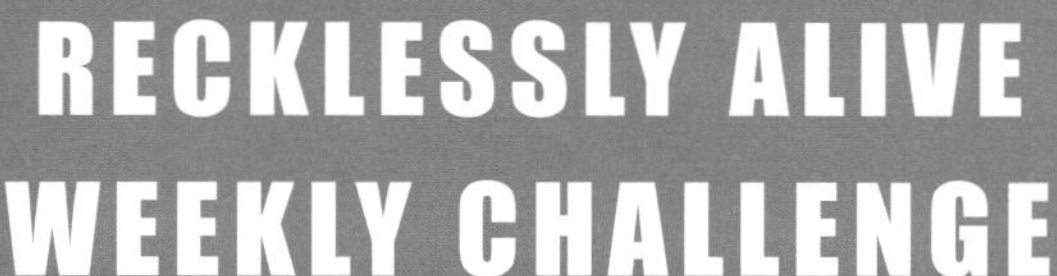

RECKLESSLY ALIVE WEEKLY CHALLENGE

What is one bold step you've hesitated to take? How can you move forward this week, trusting that growth always begins at the edge of comfort? It doesn't have to be a giant leap yet, just one real step. If you've been dreaming about writing a book, open a blank page. If you want to start running, lace up your shoes. Do the first doable thing, and let that be enough for today.

TAKE A RISK FOR YOUR FUTURE

I WAS STRAPPED TO A STRANGER WHO SMELLED LIKE AXE BODY spray and beef jerky, and the plane door was open. Twelve thousand five hundred feet below, a snow-covered landscape stretched to the horizon. My knees knocked together as the wind screamed into the cabin. Every nerve in my body begged me not to move. I was about to jump, and I had no idea why I'd said yes.

But the fear of leaping? It was nothing compared to the regret I knew I'd feel if I stayed in that plane.

I'd never been a risk-taker. I avoided discomfort. I played it safe. But that jump was one of the boldest and best things I've ever done. Somewhere in that free fall, I learned something I've never forgotten: Growth doesn't happen in comfort; it comes when you stretch, when you let go of the safety net, when you trust yourself to land.

For years, I kept my dreams locked away because they felt too big, too unrealistic, too risky. Fear whispered, *Stay small. Don't gamble with the unknown.* And for a long time, I listened.

But the moments that stay with you, the ones that shape you, aren't the safe ones. They're the leaps. The ones that make your stomach drop. The ones that test your courage and stretch your capacity.

There's a version of you, someone braver and wiser, looking back at you from the future. They've lived through the leap you're afraid to take. And if they could speak into this moment, they'd say, *Thank you. Thank you for trusting me enough to go for it. The fear and discomfort were worth it.*

The regret we carry isn't usually from falling; it's from staying still and from letting fear tether us to a life that's too small.

Growth is uncomfortable, but it's also freeing. When you say yes to the unknown, when you dare to stretch beyond what feels manageable, you open the door to the life you were made for.

So take the risk. Feel the fear. Let it be there and move anyway. I'm not telling you to go skydiving. But I *am* telling you this:

The life you want?

It's waiting on the other side of the jump.

RECKLESSLY ALIVE AFFIRMATION

I AM BRAVE ENOUGH TO STEP INTO DISCOMFORT,
KNOWING IT'S THE PATH TO THE LIFE I LONG FOR.

REFLECTION

What is your future self hoping you'll say yes to right now? What would it look like to trust that version of you enough to take one step forward today?

You can do this.

WORDS OF ENCOURAGEMENT FROM YOUR FUTURE SELF

YOU'RE STANDING IN FRONT OF THE MIRROR, STARING AT THE reflection of someone who feels defeated. The weight of your day presses down on you, and all you can hear is the harsh whisper of your inner voice telling you you're not enough. *Lazy*, it says. *Weak. Why can't I keep it together?* The words sting, digging into the raw parts of you that are already struggling. You wonder if anyone else feels this way or silently carries the same heavy load.

Self-talk bridges who we are now and who we're becoming. But far too often, we turn our voice into a weapon during the hardest seasons. When we need grace, we offer ourselves criticism. When we're overwhelmed, we call ourselves pathetic. When life feels like too much, we tell ourselves we're not enough. But what if that inner voice could be a lifeline instead? Imagine a conversation across time where the future version of you whispers through the noise, steady and wise, reminding you that you're doing better than you think.

Imagine hearing that supportive voice telling you that every step you take, each small act of kindness toward yourself, is paving the way for the person you're becoming. Your future self wouldn't judge you for this moment. They'd hold space for you, acknowledging your persistence and strength, even when it feels like you're losing. "Keep going," they'd say. "You're closer than you think."

There's beauty in thinking of self-talk as hearing from your future self, a reminder that you are worthy of care and patience, despite feeling like you're far from it. If you could meet the version of you who's already lived through this, they'd smile, knowing that these difficult moments made you strong. They'd look back at you with the deepest compassion, saying, "I know it's hard now, but you're building something worth having. Keep going. In time, you'll be proud of the progress you've made."

Trust that voice. It's waiting for you, not in some distant future but right on the other side of this moment, ready to meet you with open arms.

RECKLESSLY ALIVE AFFIRMATION

I TRUST THAT THE PERSON I AM BECOMING IS SHAPED BY THE CHOICES I MAKE TODAY.

REFLECTION

How can you shift your self-talk from criticism to compassion today? What would it look like if you imagined your future self offering you kindness and encouragement in this moment?

You can do this.

CREATE YOUR FUTURE WORTH TODAY

THERE'S A VERSION OF YOU IN THE FUTURE THAT NO LONGER wastes energy questioning their worth. They still have bad days, but they don't spiral. They've stopped measuring their value by what they produce or how much praise they receive. They've grown into something steadier, someone who can hold the mirror and say, "This person matters."

But that version of you won't appear overnight. It will come from the result of the choices you're making right now. Each time you speak gently to yourself when it would be easier to tear yourself down. Every time you show up as you are, not as who you think you're supposed to be. Every time you whisper, *Maybe I don't have to earn love today*, you're laying the foundation for a self-worth that endures.

Living recklessly alive has nothing to do with fixing every broken piece or proving that you deserve love. Instead, it invites you to welcome the whole, unfinished you with all the doubt, fear, and healing-in-progress, and to know that even here, you are already enough.

You don't have to wait to grow into that steadier version of yourself. You're already becoming that person by choosing to stay true to who you are. One day, when that future you looks back, they'll be proud of how you kept going—not to prove anything but because you believed it was worth taking one more step toward becoming someone who no longer questions their worth.

RECKLESSLY ALIVE AFFIRMATION

I DON'T HAVE TO EARN MY WORTH.
I AM ALREADY ENOUGH, EVEN IN THE BECOMING.

REFLECTION

When do you question your worth most, and what would it look like to meet that moment with compassion instead of criticism? What small act could you take this week to move closer to the version of you who no longer doubts their value?

You can do this.

DAY 67

THE GRIT OF YOUR FUTURE IS BUILT TODAY

AT FOURTEEN I SPENT MY AFTERNOONS BAGGING GROCERIES under the glow of fluorescent lights. Life felt heavy in ways I couldn't yet name, and money was tight. The days seemed long—schoolbooks in one hand, a time card in the other—and the nights blurred into homework and exhaustion. There was no glamour in pushing carts or stocking shelves, but I showed up. I thought I might as well give it everything I had while there.

What originally seemed like monotony turned out to be a blessing. That job became more than just a paycheck. It became a rhythm amid the chaos. I worked there for more than a decade, earning vacation time and returning every college break to make ends meet.

Aside from the money, the real gift that those years gave me was resilience, the kind built in the small, unnoticed moments like mopping floors, braving winter winds to collect carts, and staying patient when someone rushed through my line without so much as a glance. That effort laid the foundation for grit—a secret advantage when life presented me with challenges far bigger than having enough money to buy groceries.

If my fourteen-year-old self could hear from me now, I'd tell him this: I know you're tired. I know this feels like just another shift, another day to get through. But what you're building now, steadily, wholeheartedly, without applause, will carry you through far more than you can see. Every cart you push, each shelf you stock, and every time you choose to care, even when no one else does, you're learning a resilience many never develop, you're building the kind of fortitude that will hold you steady when life gets harder, and you're doing so much better than you know.

Maybe you've never bagged groceries, but you know what it means to keep going when you're tired, or to show up even when no one sees the effort it takes. This type of grit isn't built in the spotlight. It's shaped in the ordinary, the exhausting, the thankless moments that ask for your patience and persistence.

If today feels like a grind, take heart. The future version of you, the one who will reap the rewards of your perseverance, is cheering you on, whispering, *Keep going.*

RECKLESSLY ALIVE AFFIRMATION

I HONOR THE RESILIENCE I'M BUILDING TODAY, KNOWING IT'S SHAPING A FUTURE I'LL BE PROUD OF.

REFLECTION

What's one moment in your life that seemed small at the time but grew into something meaningful? How can you trust the effort you're putting in today to shape your tomorrow?

You can do this.

CARE FOR THE FUTURE YOU

YOU FEEL IT BEFORE IT HITS: THE TIGHTNESS IN YOUR SHOULDers, the way your jaw clenches, that familiar churn in your stomach as your mind starts rehearsing everything that could go wrong. Maybe it's a deadline creeping closer. Maybe it's a conversation you've been dreading. The stress hasn't landed yet, but your body already senses: *Something heavy is on the way.*

You might think, *I'll deal with it when it comes*, but what if you didn't wait for the pressure to hit you full force? What if you could plan for it so that you already have a solid foundation to keep you grounded when the stress arrives?

One of my therapists once taught me a skill she called *coping ahead*, which is recognizing when challenging situations are coming and then planning how you'll support yourself through them. Think of it as packing an emotional emergency kit, not with bandages or granola bars but with whatever helps you stay steady. Maybe you plan time to unwind after a big event, leave yourself a note of encouragement to read on a tough day, ensure that you have a quiet space to retreat to, or take five minutes to cuddle your pet before returning to the mayhem.

Coping ahead is more than just preparation; it's a promise to yourself that you'll be there when it matters. You don't need to control every detail or erase the stress completely. What matters most is giving yourself what you'll need when the pressure starts to build: tools, reminders, and moments of steadiness that help you breathe through the overwhelm.

When the stress passes, and it always does, you'll look back and realize that the real gift you gave yourself was the assurance that would show up for yourself, even before you needed it.

RECKLESSLY ALIVE AFFIRMATION

I CHOOSE TO CARE FOR MYSELF WITH INTENTION AND LOVE.

REFLECTION

What challenges are coming up that could use a little prep work? How can you create a plan that helps you feel more supported when things get heavy?

You can do this.

IF YOU COULD STEP BACK INTO TODAY

ONE DAY, THIS MIGHT ALL FEEL LIKE A DREAM. THE MESSY kitchen. The sound of footsteps in the hallway. The scent of your coffee beside a half-read book. A text from someone who still knows your heart. Years from now, a version of you may give anything to step back into a day like today, not because it was easy but because it was yours. They'll remember the rhythms of now, the people who were beside you, and the small joys you've barely noticed in the rush. They're not asking you to love every second, just to notice it. To feel what's here before it slips away.

It's easy to forget how quickly time moves. We stay focused on what's next, convinced that happiness lives just past the next milestone. But life doesn't wait. The days may feel long, but the years blur faster than you expect, like a dream softening at the edges. Eventually, the version of you who's lived beyond this chapter will see what's hard to grasp now: Joy isn't always something you chase. Often, it's something you find by standing still.

Your future self sees how hard you're trying. They know what you're carrying, even if no one else does. And still, they'd remind you that what matters most usually isn't big or loud. Your greatest purpose is often found in the pause, in noticing what's right in front of you. The laughter. The light. The quiet spaces in between.

You don't have to change the world today in order to live with purpose. Sometimes living recklessly alive is found in noticing the moments you'll wish you had back someday.

RECKLESSLY ALIVE AFFIRMATION

I CHOOSE TO NOTICE THE GOOD IN THIS MOMENT.

REFLECTION

What is one thing about today you can fully savor, just as it is? How can you remind yourself that joy is already here and waiting to be noticed?

You can do this.

DAY 70

A FUTURE OF MEANINGFUL RELATIONSHIPS

I HUDDLED AT THE BACK OF THE CROWDED FUNERAL, THE SCENT of fading lilies mixing with the sharp bite of cold air every time the door opened. Around me, faces were heavy with grief: eyes puffy, tissues crumpled, hands clutching coffee cups more for comfort than caffeine. One by one, people stood to share stories, their voices unsteady but full of love. What struck me most wasn't the significant milestones people spoke of but the small moments.

Nobody talked about what kind of car she drove or how clean her house was. They talked about the way she'd make you feel like you were the only one in the room, even when it was packed. The warmth in her voice when she asked, "How are you, *really*?" as if she were waiting for something deeper than a casual response. The selflessness in the way she gave back to those around her. It wasn't her awards or achievements but the relentless way she showed up for others.

Listening to those stories, I realized that one day my future self would look back and understand the weight of those small moments for what they truly were: the foundation of everything that matters. A funeral has a way of making it clear how short our time really is and how much those gestures shape the legacy we leave behind.

So make the call. Send the message. Make someone feel seen and heard. Tell the people you love how much they mean to you while they're still here. Because connection isn't something you stumble upon; it's something you build, piece by piece, one small gesture at a time.

When the time comes for others to speak your name in a cemetery, they won't talk about what you owned. They'll talk about how you made them feel. They'll remember the love you gave away in a thousand small moments, and that will be what endures.

RECKLESSLY ALIVE AFFIRMATION

I PRIORITIZE CONNECTION, KNOWING THAT EACH SMALL ACT OF LOVE AND CARE HELPS BUILD A MEANINGFUL LIFE.

REFLECTION

Who in your life might need a little more attention right now? How can you show up for them, even in a small way, today?

You can do this.

WEEK 11

MOMENTS THAT MATTER

LIFE ISN'T DEFINED BY THE MOMENTS WE PLAN; IT'S SHAPED BY the moments we choose to embrace fully. Living in the moment invites us to be present, even when fear or uncertainty threatens to pull us away. We can say yes to opportunities that stretch us, knowing that they can shift our perspective to see the good in challenges and trusting that each small, intentional choice can create a more vibrant and meaningful life.

This week, we'll explore what it looks like to live in the moment. From facing fears and rewriting your inner dialogue to building authentic connections, each step brings you closer to a life rooted in purpose and joy. This is your invitation to let go of distractions, lean in to the present, and discover the power of fully living—right here, right now.

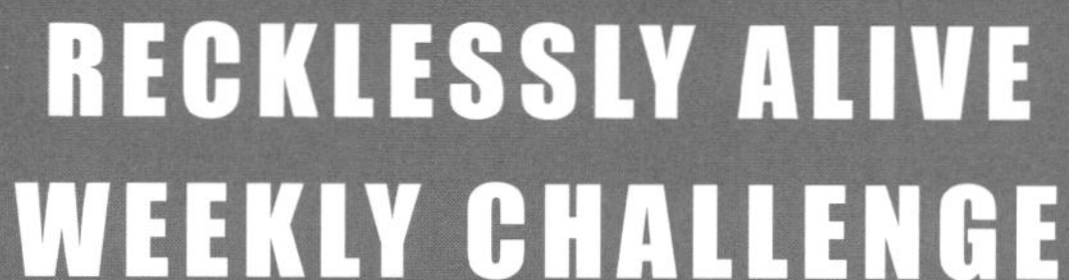

Think of a time when you witnessed someone being hurt but you stayed silent. This week, look for a moment that matters—an opportunity to use your voice to stand up, speak kindness, or offer support. It doesn't have to be big to be brave. Let this be the week you choose courage over silence.

SPEAK UP WHEN IT MATTERS

THE GYM WAS ALIVE WITH EXCITEMENT, THE AIR FILLED WITH THE aroma of popcorn and the sound of the crowd cheering. I sat in the bleachers, lost in the energy of the pep fest, when I suddenly heard it: a group of boys behind me, laughing, their voices sharp and cruel as one of them hurled a slur. I turned slightly to see who they were talking about, and there he was, sitting a few rows ahead. His shoulders were tense, his eyes were cast down, and he was doing everything he could to make himself invisible. I could see the hurt in his face, the pain of being targeted.

The boys behind me kept laughing, repeatedly hurling words at him. My heart sank as I watched him struggle to stay composed. I knew I should have said something in that moment, but I stayed frozen. The words caught in my throat, and instead of standing up for him, I stayed silent, feeling my shame build as the laughter continued. I felt a tightness in my chest that wouldn't disappear, and the remorse settled in.

I will forever regret not defending that boy. Standing up for someone isn't always easy; it's messy and vulnerable. It might come at a cost. But when we act or speak up for what's right, even when it feels uncomfortable, those moments matter.

I've lived with the weight of not standing up for someone who needed me, and it's a regret I still carry with me. But I learned from that experience and no longer let those moments slip by. Now I speak up for those near me who need someone to defend them. I seek out the marginalized around me and lend them my strength when they are in need. And I'll continue to do so, because the moments when we choose to act, even when it's hard or scary, are the ones that truly matter.

If you ever hear a harmful comment, you don't need to have a perfect speech ready. Some days all it takes is a steady voice saying, "That's not okay," or "Don't talk that way," or even "Hey, are you all right?" to the person it was aimed at. It might feel awkward. You might fumble. But your words have power, and they might be what someone else needs to feel seen, supported, and safe.

So look for those moments this week. Seek out the person sitting alone. Call out the cruelty in the joke. Offer backup when someone is being mistreated. These small choices add up. Because the moments that matter most are the ones when you decide to use your voice.

RECKLESSLY ALIVE AFFIRMATION

I CHOOSE TO SPEAK UP AND ADVOCATE FOR OTHERS, KNOWING THAT MY VOICE CAN MAKE A DIFFERENCE.

REFLECTION

Is there a moment when you stayed silent that still sits heavy in your heart? How can you choose to respond differently the next time someone needs your voice?

You can do this.

DAY 72

THE COMPLIMENTS THAT MATTER

I WAS STROLLING THROUGH THE BRIGHT, ECHOEY GATHERING space of a modern church I'd never been to before. The scent of vanilla coffee creamer hung in the air and mixed with the damp warmth of a soft spring rain that still clung to people's jackets. I was in town to speak on a podcast and knew only one person in the entire city. She'd invited me to her church that morning, but I couldn't find her. I stood still for a moment amid the low chatter of unfamiliar conversations and felt even more alone than usual.

I wandered aimlessly, unsure of where to go or who to talk to, until an elderly woman walked past. She wore a teal blazer and gold earrings that caught the light when she turned her head. Our eyes met, and I gave a small, polite smile—more out of habit than joy. She stepped toward me, touched my arm gently, and said, "Your smile lights up this entire room."

That's all she said. Then she moved on. But I still hear her voice sometimes when I smile, like a little reminder that maybe I bring more light into the world than I realize.

We focus a lot on *self*-talk, and that's important. But the manner in which we speak to ourselves is shaped by the voices we've encountered along the way. Some words left wounds. Others, like hers, left healing. That one compliment became a kind of anchor for me. I found myself smiling more, not because everything was better but because someone saw something good in me, and I decided to believe her.

You never know which words will create the moment that matters. The ones that interrupt the spiral. The ones someone holds on to for years. So maybe today, say the kind thing. Offer the compliment. Speak the truth someone might need to hear.

And when your inner critic shows up again, dragging out all its old lines, try borrowing hers. Let it echo. Let it soften something in you.

You matter, exactly as you are. Maybe you just need to hear it again.

RECKLESSLY ALIVE AFFIRMATION

THE KINDNESS I OFFER TO MYSELF AND OTHERS HAS LASTING IMPACT. I WILL SPEAK WORDS THAT HEAL AND UPLIFT.

REFLECTION

What's one kind sentence someone has said to you that has stayed with you? How might you pay that kindness forward today?

You can do this.

NO APOLOGY NEEDED

THE CEILING FANS SPUN LAZILY OVERHEAD, STIRRING THE SMELL of sizzling bacon and burnt toast through the crowded diner. Plates clattered in the kitchen, and the booths were alive with the low buzz of conversation and clinking coffee mugs. I was five minutes late to meet a friend for lunch and had spent the entire drive beating myself up over it. As I slid into the red corner booth, the first words out of my mouth were, "I'm so sorry."

My friend glanced up from the menu, unfazed. "You're good. I just got here."

Still, I felt that familiar knot in my stomach, like I had done something wrong and needed to earn my way back into good graces for being human. It wasn't about the time; it was about the story I'd told myself on the drive over: that I was inconsiderate, scattered, always letting people down.

It hit me later that I do this all the time. I apologize when I ask a question. When I speak up in a group. When I need more time to respond to a message. It's like a reflex, an apology for existing.

Of course we should offer sincere apologies when we've hurt someone or made a real mistake. But there's a difference between being accountable and constantly shrinking to stay likable. Chronic apologizing doesn't make you more thoughtful; it chips away at your self-worth.

The moments that matter are often the ones when we pause and choose differently. When we say, "Thanks for waiting," instead of saying, "Sorry I'm late." When we ask for help without shame. When we speak our needs clearly without minimizing them first.

Try these swaps the next time the urge to over-apologize sneaks in:

Instead of saying, "Sorry for bothering you," try, "Do you have a moment?"

Instead of saying, "Sorry I'm a mess," try, "Thanks for being patient with me today."

Instead of saying, "Sorry I'm not making sense," try, "Let me start again."

Every time you catch yourself before a needless apology, you're making a silent declaration: *I belong. I'm allowed to take up space. I don't have to apologize for being human.*

RECKLESSLY ALIVE AFFIRMATION

I DON'T NEED TO SHRINK MYSELF TO BE ACCEPTED.

REFLECTION

What's one situation this week where you felt the urge to over-apologize? How can you practice replacing that habit with self-compassion or gratitude?

You can do this.

CARRY FEAR AND MOVE FORWARD

THE PANIC HIT FAST, LIKE IT ALWAYS DOES. I WAS SITTING IN MY car, keys still in the ignition, when the wave rolled over me. Chest tight. Palms slick. That strange heat that rushes up your neck and makes it hard to breathe. I gripped the steering wheel, frozen in place, brain spinning through a hundred worst-case scenarios. I felt like I was disappearing, swallowed whole by something I couldn't name.

A few weeks earlier, my therapist had given me a tool for moments like this: "Keep sour candy in your glove box," she said. "And when you feel it coming on, pop one in your mouth and rub the center of your chest. Slow circles. Right over the sternum." It sounded ridiculous. But that day in the car, I was desperate. I did exactly what she had told me, and slowly, the edge started to dull.

The panic didn't vanish. But something shifted when I did something different. I didn't spiral all the way down. I reached for a tool instead of collapsing under the weight of the stress. And that changed something in me.

The moments that matter are often the ones where you decide to do something new. When you recognize a familiar spiral and choose a different response. When you try the breathing technique. When you speak the hard thing out loud. When you find a healthy way to release your emotions instead of numbing them. This is radical self-love in action, proof that you're showing up for yourself in a new way, even when it's hard.

So whatever you're facing today—whether it's panic you're trying to overcome or a feeling you're learning to sit with—I hope you remember this: Reaching for a new tool is a sign you're developing resilience. Trying something new when everything inside you wants to shut down—that's a moment that matters. It doesn't have to *look* brave to *be* brave. Just take the next breath. Reach for the thing that might help. That's enough.

RECKLESSLY ALIVE AFFIRMATION

I AM LEARNING NEW WAYS TO CARE FOR MYSELF. EACH TOOL I REACH FOR IS A REMINDER OF MY STRENGTH AND RESILIENCE.

REFLECTION

What's one strategy or tool you've tried, or one you want to try, the next time you face a tough moment? How can you practice reaching for it when you need it most?

You can do this.

WHEN YOU OWN IT INSTEAD OF SPIRALING

THE SUN HAD JUST DIPPED BEHIND THE TREES, CASTING LONG shadows across the quiet street. I had pulled into a neighborhood I didn't know well while juggling a long to-do list among my racing thoughts. And that's when it happened: I backed into a parked car.

The crunch of bumper against bumper stopped me cold. My heart dropped into my stomach. That unmistakable wave of embarrassment hit, fast and hot. I sat frozen, overwhelmed with how stupid I felt. The voice in my head grew aggressive: *How could I be so careless? What's wrong with me?*

I wanted to disappear. But instead, I did something different. I got out of my car and looked around for the other car's owner. I left a note with my number and details. I called my insurance company. And then, because I process life by talking about it, I posted online. I wrote about how small and ridiculous I felt, how I was choosing not to spiral in shame, how I was allowed to make a mistake without punishing myself for days.

What happened next surprised me. That post was flooded with stories from people who'd done the exact same thing. People who said it made them feel less alone. People who thanked me for being honest about something they usually hide.

It hit me: This wasn't just about taking responsibility. It was about choosing how I show up for myself when I mess up. That's self-care too. Not just bubble baths or boundaries or journaling but deciding not to berate myself over a human mistake. Choosing grace over shame. Action over avoidance. Ownership over spiraling.

The moments that matter aren't always the ones we plan for. Some days they show up in the form of a dented bumper and a choice to be kind to yourself anyway.

RECKLESSLY ALIVE AFFIRMATION

I AM ALLOWED TO MAKE MISTAKES AND LEARN FROM THEM.

REFLECTION

Think back to a time when you made a mistake. How did you treat yourself afterward? How might self-care look different if you respond with compassion instead of criticism?

You can do this.

A MOMENT TO LOVE A STRANGER

THE PLANE WAS OVERBOOKED AND OVERHEATED WITH THE KIND of stifling warmth that makes you second-guess wearing a hoodie. I was wiped out, having barely slept the night before. I tucked my head against the window, ready to disappear. Then came the scream.

A toddler, red-faced, kicking, and inconsolable, was being carried down the aisle by his flustered mom, diaper bag slipping from her shoulder, apologies spilling from her mouth. They stopped at my row, of course.

I gave a stingy smile and shifted my things to give them space. The mom tried everything: snacks, toys, gentle shushing. Nothing worked, and the crying intensified. The people around us sighed and turned up their headphones. I sat frozen, torn between frustration and sympathy, trying to will myself invisible. And then he looked at me.

His little face was blotchy and tear streaked, but when our eyes met, he paused. Just for a second. I waved awkwardly. He didn't smile, but he stopped screaming. A few minutes later, he crawled onto my lap.

His mom panicked, eyes wide. "I'm so sorry."

"It's okay," I said, settling him into the crook of my arm.

He stayed with for me most of the flight. We flipped through the safety card, drew shapes on a napkin, and shared a pack of crackers. Eventually, he fell asleep on my chest, and for the first time since takeoff, the cabin exhaled. Helping that mom have two hours of relief felt like the most important thing I could've done that day.

Purpose doesn't always look like changing the world, especially to the outsider who may only see you helping a stranger through a hard moment or checking in on an elderly neighbor. But meaning often lives in the ordinary, waiting for someone willing to notice.

Today, I hope you keep your eyes open. Maybe there's a mom who needs ten minutes alone to drink her coffee. A neighbor who needs a ride. A friend who just needs an ear. The moments that matter don't usually announce themselves, but when you respond with compassion and empathy, you're living on purpose.

RECKLESSLY ALIVE AFFIRMATION

I LIVE WITH PURPOSE WHEN I CHOOSE TO CARE. EVEN SMALL ACTS OF KINDNESS CAN OFFER RELIEF, CONNECTION, AND LOVE.

REFLECTION

Who around you might need a break, a breath, or a little support? What's one way you can help someone else carry what they're holding today?

You can do this.

DAY 77

WHEN IT'S TIME TO LET GO

THE SCENT OF SIMMERING CHILI HUNG IN THE AIR AND MINGLED with the fragrance of the tart, cold cider I held in my hand as I stepped out onto the deck. Beanbags thudded against cornhole boards, and laughter rose from the kitchen where old friends caught up like no time had passed.

Except time *had* passed. A lot of it.

I looked around at the people who had once been my second family, sharing bonfires, weekend trips, late-night heart-to-hearts. Back then, we were inseparable. Now life looked different. Marriages. Babies. Group texts gone silent. Entire conversations built around nap schedules and feeding routines. None of it wrong, just new.

For a while, I held on to what we used to be, wondering how to get back there. But standing on that deck, I realized that I didn't need to. What we had then mattered deeply, and what we have now matters, too, even if it was softer, quieter, less constant.

Friendships evolve. Maybe that means fewer hangouts, shorter conversations, and long stretches of silence. But that doesn't mean the connection is gone; it might ust be changing shape. The moments that matter might not look like weekend road trips anymore. Instead, they might look like a voice memo on a busy morning. A quick hug at a birthday party. A knowing glance across a crowded room.

I used to grieve what we'd lost. Now I'm learning to honor what still remains.

The truth is, connection shows up in small, steady ways. And when you look back, those are the moments that still matter.

RECKLESSLY ALIVE AFFIRMATION

I CAN HONOR THE PAST WITHOUT STAYING STUCK IN IT.

REFLECTION

Is there a relationship, group, or version of your life you've outgrown? What would it look like to thank it for what it gave you and then to gently let it go?

You can do this.

WEEK 12

BECOMING WHO YOU'RE MEANT TO BE

BECOMING WHO YOU'RE MEANT TO BE DOESN'T MEAN YOU HAVE to reinvent yourself overnight. By uncovering the parts of you that have always been there—your dreams, strengths, and light—you can choose to live in alignment with them. This might look like having the courage to say yes to big opportunities, the compassion to meet yourself where you are, or the determination to rewrite the story you no longer want to live.

This week, we'll explore what it means to embrace your unique path. Whether it's dreaming big, taking bold steps, letting go of self-doubt, or building deeper connections, every moment shapes the person you're becoming. Perfection was never the goal. What matters is showing up fully, with authenticity, purpose, and the confidence that you're exactly where you need to be.

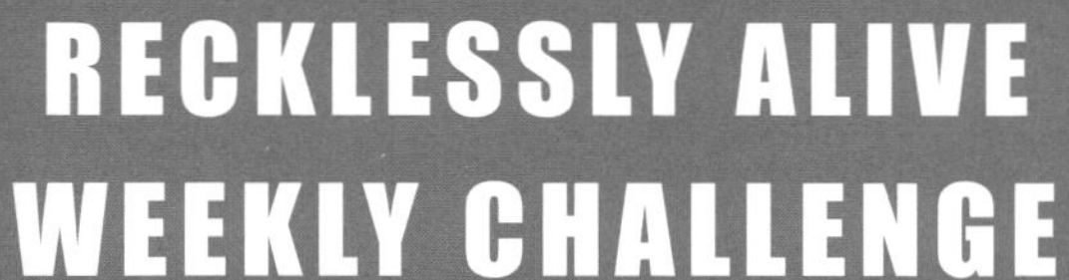

RECKLESSLY ALIVE WEEKLY CHALLENGE

Write a letter to the version of you that you're becoming. What do you hope future you remembers, releases, or finally believes about themselves? Seal it and keep it somewhere safe.

You're not waiting to become someone else; you're uncovering who you've been all along.

BECOME BRAVE ENOUGH TO DREAM

THE EMAIL ARRIVED LATE AT NIGHT, AND MY HEART WAS RACING when I finished reading it. A six-week trip to Zimbabwe with a group of musicians, playing in schools, connecting with students, and immersing ourselves in a different world. It sounded like something out of a movie—too big, too extraordinary, too impossible for someone like me. Then I got to the bottom of the page and saw the cost: thousands of dollars I didn't have.

I almost closed my laptop right then and there, but a small, stubborn voice inside whispered, *What if I try?*

Over the next few weeks, I threw myself into the challenge. I wrote heartfelt letters to friends and family, sharing my dream and asking for their support. I sold baked goods, hosted a garage sale, and played my guitar at any event that would have me. My confidence grew with every dollar raised, though the doubt never fully left. *What if I can't pull it off? What if I fail?*

There were moments when I felt like giving up, wondering if I was foolish to believe that I could make it work. But every yes I received reminded me why I was doing this: I wasn't only chasing a dream; I was stepping into the person I wanted to become.

When we finally landed in Zimbabwe, I felt overwhelmed by the vibrant rhythm of life there. The music, the laughter, and the kindness were unlike anything I'd ever experienced. Playing for kids whose joy radiated despite so much hardship was humbling. And somehow, through every note played and every smile shared, I found pieces of myself I didn't know were missing.

Dreaming big comes with no guarantees. It asks you to believe in something so deeply that you're willing to face the discomfort, the fear, and the unknown to bring it to life. Becoming who you're meant to be often starts with a thought that says, *Yes, I might fail, but try anyway.*

If something is tugging at your heart, give it a chance, no matter how impossible it seems. The world needs your boldness, your creativity, and your willingness to take that first step. Each step forward, even an uncertain one, has the power to lead you somewhere fuller, truer, and more beautiful than you ever imagined.

RECKLESSLY ALIVE AFFIRMATION

I AM BRAVE ENOUGH TO DREAM BIG AND TAKE BOLD STEPS TOWARD BECOMING WHO I'M MEANT TO BE.

REFLECTION

What's one belief, fear, or story you're ready to leave behind as you take the next step toward that most authentic version of you?

You can do this.

BECOME YOUR OWN ALLY

I SAT AT THE EDGE OF MY UNMADE BED, HALF DRESSED FOR THE day, holding a sock in my hand like I'd forgotten what to do with it. The morning light slanted through the blinds, dust catching in the air. Everything felt heavy: my to-do list, my unanswered messages, and the ache in my chest I couldn't quite explain. I sat on the edge of the bed, elbows on knees, fingers tangled in my hair.

The room was quiet, but my thoughts were screaming. That voice again, the one that knew exactly where to aim. Every criticism and every insult I'd ever absorbed came rushing back like they'd just been waiting for this moment. I tried to shake them off, to push them down, but they kept coming: *I'm a mess. I'll never get it together. Why can't I just be better? I'm lazy. I'm behind. I'm never going to figure this out.* Each line hit like a punch. I didn't move; I just stared at the floor, wondering how something as simple as getting dressed could feel like a mountain.

I hadn't realized how loud the lies had become, how long I'd been treating myself like someone undeserving of grace.

If hating yourself worked, you'd already have everything you ever wanted. But the truth is, no one ever hated themself into a better life. That inner voice, the one that clings to your mistakes and constantly whispers that you're not enough, is not protecting you. It's holding you back.

Being kind to your mind means showing up for yourself

with honesty and gentleness, even on the hard days. Facing the messiest parts of yourself and saying, *This is where I begin*, takes real courage. Remind yourself that you don't need to have it all together to deserve kindness, whether it's your own or someone else's.

Each act of self-kindness, no matter how small, is a step toward becoming who you're meant to be.

So when that voice tries to tell you you're not enough, answer it. Not with false cheer or empty reassurances but with the quiet truth: *I'm doing my best right now. Even though I am not perfect, I am here, and that is enough.*

You don't have to be perfect to begin healing; you just have to stop being your own enemy and start becoming your own ally.

RECKLESSLY ALIVE AFFIRMATION

I DON'T HAVE TO HATE MYSELF INTO CHANGE.
I CHOOSE COMPASSION, KNOWING THAT
KINDNESS IS WHAT HELPS ME GROW.

REFLECTION

What would it look like to meet yourself with gentleness today? What's one kind thing you can do for or say to yourself to become your own ally?

You can do this.

YOU ARE ENOUGH WITHOUT THEIR APPROVAL

I REMEMBER DRIVING FOR EIGHT HOURS, WITH SNACKS SHOVED in the center console and a carefully curated playlist humming through the speakers—just to spend a weekend catching up with her. We'd sit at a little brunch spot near her place, sip weak diner coffee, and talk about our dreams like no time had passed.

Over the years, I made a lot of those trips. I booked flights. Sent birthday gifts. Showed up for family events. Gave rides to the airport when needed. I carved time out of busy seasons because I believed that that's what love looks like. You show up. And I don't regret that. But I can't deny what slowly built up under the surface.

She never made the trip to see me. Never initiated plans. Never checked in when things in my world were falling apart. I kept telling myself that she cared in her own way. I made excuses for the silence, for the one-word texts, for how the conversation always shifted back to her.

One day, without much ceremony, I decided to stop initiating to see what would happen. Six months passed. Nothing. Not a call. Not a text.

I'd be lying if I said it didn't sting. Not just because I missed her but because I had to face a hard truth: I had been pouring into a friendship that didn't pour back. Somewhere along the way, I had convinced myself that being a "good friend" meant never asking for anything in return. But that's not friendship; that's self-abandonment dressed up as loyalty.

Relationships are rarely perfectly balanced. There are seasons when one person gives more than the other. But love—true, mutual love—doesn't leave you wondering if you matter.

Part of becoming who you're meant to be is learning when to hold on with both hands and when to loosen your grip. It's learning to value yourself enough to recognize when someone has stopped showing up for you, and deciding that you won't keep shrinking just to stay connected.

You are not too much for wanting mutual effort. You are worthy of people who choose you too.

RECKLESSLY ALIVE AFFIRMATION

I AM WORTHY OF FRIENDSHIPS ROOTED IN MUTUAL CARE, EFFORT, AND RESPECT. I WILL NO LONGER SETTLE FOR BEING THE ONLY ONE WHO SHOWS UP.

REFLECTION

Which relationships in your life feel balanced or unbalanced? How might life feel different if you prioritized connections that were more mutual?

You can do this.

PUSH THROUGH THE FEAR

THE BACKYARD WAS STRUNG WITH TWINKLE LIGHTS, AND THE smell of grilled burgers drifted through the humid summer air. A small group of people sat scattered on picnic blankets and folding chairs, laughing and swatting at mosquitoes. I stood behind the mic stand, clutching my notes with clammy hands, trying to slow my breath.

I didn't want to be there. I was preparing to give my first speech, microphone in hand, ready to share my story during a concert intermission. The speech was about mental-health awareness, a cause close to my heart, but as I stood there, the fear hit me in full force. I could still feel the rush of panic from when I had pulled over on the way to the event to dry heave in a ditch. My stomach still churned with the feelings that I was unqualified, underprepared, and wildly out of place. My mind screamed, *I'm not ready! I don't belong here!*

But when the host called my name, I walked forward anyway.

I could feel my legs shaking. The words I'd practiced slipped away for a moment, and I froze. But then something clicked: I didn't need to be perfect; I just needed to speak. The words slowly began to come. I wasn't simply talking; I was sharing my truth, my own struggle with mental health, and the importance of speaking up.

Resilience isn't something you either have or you don't; it's something you build. Like a muscle, it grows each time you choose to keep going when everything in you wants to give up. That first speech didn't feel like resilience. It felt like panic and nausea and a desperate wish to disappear. But what I couldn't see then was that showing up anyway was the beginning of a strength I didn't know I had.

Eight years and over two hundred events later, I don't really get nervous anymore. But that's not because I'm fearless; it's because I've practiced. I've messed up. I've learned. And I've kept showing up. Everyone who is where you want to be started with a shaky, nervous first step. The question isn't whether you'll feel ready. The question is whether you'll keep going when you don't.

So wherever you are today, facing something new, uncomfortable, or hard, remember that this might be the rep that makes you stronger. You don't have to feel brave to build resilience. You just need to stay in it. Trust the process. Keep showing up. That's how we become who we're meant to be.

RECKLESSLY ALIVE AFFIRMATION

I DON'T HAVE TO BE FEARLESS; I JUST
NEED TO KEEP SHOWING UP.

REFLECTION

What's something you're doing right now that stretches you? What would it look like to treat that challenge as something that's growing your resilience?

You can do this.

DAY 82

GROW AMID THE BOREDOM

THE WORLD IS ADDICTED TO NOISE. EVERYWHERE WE LOOK, something is competing for our attention—notifications, endless streams of updates, and conversations that never seem to end. We've grown so used to filling each moment with activity that stillness feels almost unnatural. But in the rush to stay busy, a lot of us fill our days with noise so we don't have to sit with the hard stuff. But when we finally stop running and face the stillness, that's where clarity can begin. Growth often starts the moment we stop hiding from ourselves.

Boredom, far from being an inconvenience, is one of the most powerful ways to reconnect with ourselves. It provides moments of stillness when we're not scrolling, not rushing, not consumed by the next thing, so we can create space to reflect. To rest. To notice the parts of us that need attention. Boredom doesn't mean idleness; it means making room for clarity and presence, things we sacrifice when we're consumed by distraction.

When distraction takes over, it becomes easy to lose track of the things that actually matter—our peace, our clarity, our sense of direction. Real self-care isn't always about adding more; sometimes it's about giving ourselves permission to pause. To step away from the noise. To stop performing and start listening to our life again. At first, the stillness can feel awkward, even a little unsettling, but that's when the real work begins. We start to notice the patterns that have been running the show. Growth isn't always comfortable, and becoming who we're meant to be often requires stepping outside the patterns that keep us stuck.

The world won't slow down for us, but we can choose to slow down for ourselves. When we step back, we reconnect with the deeper parts of us that don't need to do, achieve, or prove anything to be enough. In the quiet, we give ourselves the gift of presence, where the real work of becoming begins.

RECKLESSLY ALIVE AFFIRMATION

I HONOR MY JOURNEY BY EMBRACING STILLNESS.
I MAKE SPACE FOR REST, REFLECTION, AND GROWTH.

REFLECTION

How can you create moments of stillness in your life today? What might you discover about yourself in the space between distractions?

You can do this.

DAY 83

BECOMING BY SAYING NO

MY PHONE BUZZED NONSTOP WITH WEEKEND PLANS. SOMEONE suggested grilling at the park, someone else promised to bring s'mores, and the conversation quickly spiraled into laughter. These were good people, people I trusted. Normally, I'd be the first one to say I was in.

Yet something in me was begging to stay home this time.

I'd been moving too fast for too long, saying yes to everything, terrified of letting anyone down or missing out. But I was beyond exhausted. Not the kind of tired a nap could fix, but more like the kind that settles deep in your bones when you've been ignoring your own needs for too long.

So, surprising everyone, most of all myself, I said I couldn't make it.

Not because I didn't care about my friends, but because I needed to care for myself. I needed a weekend to breathe, to be quiet, to remember who I was when I wasn't rushing to keep up. And you know what? No one was mad. Everyone just said, "See you at the next one."

It's hard to disappoint people, especially when the invitation is to something good. But every yes costs you something: your time, your focus, your energy. And when you say yes to everything, you lose the space for the things that matter most.

Sometimes the bravest thing you can do is to say no to good

things so you have the capacity to say yes to what's meant for you. That single no seemed small in the moment, but it was the first step toward living with intention instead of exhaustion. And over time, I've learned that honoring your limits isn't weakness; it's how you make space for the life you're actually meant to live.

RECKLESSLY ALIVE AFFIRMATION

I CHOOSE MY PURPOSE BY SAYING NO WHEN NECESSARY, AND BY MAKING ROOM FOR WHAT I NEED IN ORDER TO FEEL GOOD IN MY BODY, MIND, AND SPIRIT.

REFLECTION

What's one thing you've been saying yes to that doesn't serve your true purpose? How can you begin saying no to make space for what matters?

You can do this.

HAVE COURAGE TO MAKE NEW CONNECTIONS

I WALKED INTO THE GRAND BALLROOM IN MY TUXEDO THAT FELT too tight. My stomach churned. It was one of those nights where everything seemed to shimmer with an elegance I wasn't used to. A Grammy-winning jazz player filled the air with beautiful music, his fingers dancing effortlessly over the piano keys. I had just spoken at a conference hosted by a prestigious university, and somehow I had been invited to join the evening's gathering as an esteemed guest.

But the social anxiety of not knowing anyone was screaming for me to run. But as I turned to leave, a different voice broke through, saying, *What if I try to find one, kind person?*

After a few moments of hesitation, I spotted a graceful woman in a sparkly blue dress, her kindness shining brighter than the sequins. I walked over and said, "Hi, I'm Sam. I don't know anyone here. Mind if I stand by you for a little bit?" She smiled and welcomed me into her circle, and soon began introducing me to everyone around her.

For much of my life, I let fear hold me back from moments like this. I stayed quiet, worried about saying the wrong thing, waiting for someone else to invite me in. But sometimes, building a new confidence in yourself starts with a tiny goal: *I'll find one kind person.* Or: *I'll try for ten minutes, and if it feels too hard, I can always try again another day.*

Dinner was served—perfectly seared salmon with roasted vegetables, the kind of meal that feels too beautiful to eat. Conversations at my table turned warm and easy, the kind where you're laughing one moment and nodding thoughtfully the next. As dessert plates were cleared, I quietly excused myself for an early bedtime. "It was wonderful to meet you all," I said to the new connections at my table. I walked out into the cool night air with a strange mix of calm and pride, not because I'd met my new best friend, but because I'd pushed past the fear and tried.

And I hope that when you find yourself standing at the edge of a room that feels bigger than you, you'll do the same. Take a breath. Walk up to someone and say hello. It may not change your whole life in that moment, but it will change *you,* because every small risk to connect shapes us into the person we're becoming.

RECKLESSLY ALIVE AFFIRMATION

I HAVE THE COURAGE TO SHOW UP WHEN I AM AFRAID.

REFLECTION

Think of a time when you felt out of place but chose to engage anyway. What helped you build connection in that moment, and how might you carry that courage into future interactions?

You can do this.

WEEK 13

LIVING RECKLESSLY ALIVE

THIS IS THE CULMINATION OF EVERYTHING WE'VE BEEN BUILDING in this journey together—the quiet shifts, the bold steps, and the truths we've unearthed along the way. It's what our everyday momentum has been moving toward: a sense of being truly, recklessly alive. *You Can Do This* isn't just a reminder for the hard days; it's a way of living. It's a belief we've practiced over and over, even when it felt out of reach.

Living recklessly alive invites you to step into the life that feels most honest and full for you. Not a perfect life but a meaningful one. The kind that embraces joy and pain, growth and rest, beginnings and endings. No one else can define what that looks like for you. And no one else gets to take it from you.

This week, we'll revisit the lessons that have carried you here. From dreaming big and building resilience to embracing connection and gratitude, each step has prepared you for this moment. Living recklessly alive shows up in the way you fold those lessons into your everyday life, finding courage in the chaos, purpose in the ordinary, and light in the small things. You've done the work. Now it's time to live it.

RECKLESSLY ALIVE WEEKLY CHALLENGE

Look back at the journey you've taken through these pages. Which moments challenged you, changed you, or reminded you who you are? Write down a few ways you've grown or shifted since you began. You've come farther than you think, and this is only the beginning.

CHOOSE TO BE FULLY ALIVE

THERE'S NO SINGLE BLUEPRINT FOR WHAT BOLDNESS LOOKS LIKE. Maybe it's raising your hand when you usually make yourself small. Maybe it's walking away from something good that's no longer right. Maybe it's speaking a dream into existence, knowing that it terrifies you but deciding to go after it anyway.

There's a moment right before you act when everything in you says, *Don't do it. Do what you've always done.* Your heart races, your stomach drops, and doubt floods in, begging you to turn back. But then you move. You take the step, say the words, and at that moment, you feel fear and freedom tangled together.

This entire journey has been about stepping out of survival mode and learning to live with intention. And nothing shifts your life like doing the hard thing you've been avoiding. Not because the outcome is guaranteed but because the act of choosing movement rewrites the story you're telling yourself about what's possible.

Living recklessly alive demands this kind of bravery. Not recklessness for the sake of chaos but the kind that says, *This matters to me. I want to feel awake in my life. I refuse to coast through it numb.*

So live boldly, my friend. Start where you are. Listen to the whispers of your heart. Take the risk that's been keeping you stuck. This is how you build a life that feels honest, full, and recklessly alive. You can do this, one bold action at a time.

RECKLESSLY ALIVE AFFIRMATION

I CHOOSE TO LIVE RECKLESSLY ALIVE, EMBRACING EACH STEP FORWARD AS AN ACT OF COURAGE.

REFLECTION

How have you changed since the beginning of this journey? What's one way you've shown up with more honesty, courage, or intention in your life?

You can do this.

SAY WORDS THAT HELP YOU FEEL ALIVE

HOW YOU SPEAK TO YOURSELF SHAPES EVERYTHING—YOUR courage, choices, and ability to step into the life you want. Those inner conversations aren't only background noise; they're the script that guides your days. And if you're going to live recklessly alive, that voice needs to push you forward, not hold you back.

Rewriting how we speak to ourselves isn't something that happens overnight. It's a daily decision to choose honesty over cruelty, progress over perfection. And some days it starts with just a whisper of kindness in the middle of the noise.

Think about the words you repeat in your mind. Are they filled with possibility, or are they rooted in doubt? When fear whispers, *I'm not enough*, can you answer back with something stronger, something true? *I can try. I can grow. I can get through this.* If this journey has taught you anything, I hope it's this: You don't have to let that voice run wild.

You've practiced speaking up when the old narratives creep in. You've challenged the harshness, questioned the lies, and started telling yourself the truth. You've learned how to say, *I'll go, and I'll decide when I get there.* You've started whispering kind phrases, even when you didn't believe them yet. And slowly, those words might just begin to sound less like a stranger's and more like yours.

Some mornings, I still catch myself bracing for the day like I'm walking into battle. But then I take a breath and say, *I can do this*. Even when I barely believe it (and especially then).

Let your self-talk reflect the person you're becoming—not the version shaped by shame or fear but the one building a life that feels recklessly alive. Speak to yourself like an ally, like someone worth rooting for—because you are.

So say it out loud. Say it again. Say it until it becomes your default. Let it be the voice that carries you through the doubt and the setbacks and the shaky beginnings.

You can do this.

RECKLESSLY ALIVE AFFIRMATION

I CHOOSE TO SPEAK TO MYSELF IN WAYS THAT REFLECT THE COURAGE AND POSSIBILITY WITHIN ME.

REFLECTION

What will stick with you about self-talk from this journey? How can you carry those lessons forward to create a life that feels vibrant and alive?

You can do this.

DAY 87

BE FULLY ALIVE AND WORTHY

SELF-WORTH DOESN'T NEED TO BE EARNED OR PROVEN. THIS KIND of value lives within you already, untouched by achievements, appearances, or anyone else's opinions. Even in the messiest, most uncertain moments, your worth remains whole.

The world will try to tell you otherwise. It will dangle shiny metrics of success, convincing you that your worth lies in the size of your paycheck, the number of likes on a post, or how much you can give before breaking. But living recklessly alive invites us to step off that treadmill and embody the truth that our worth was there the day we were born and hasn't wavered since.

There's a quiet kind of bravery in deciding that you matter, and in vowing to stop chasing worth in other people's reactions and to start coming home to yourself. That's what you've been practicing this whole time. And today, we name it clearly: You are worthy, and you are already enough.

You've done the hard work of untangling your identity from what you do, how you look, or how others treat you. You've questioned the old stories that said you had to prove something to deserve love. You've begun to speak to yourself with more kindness, grace, and truth. And now you get to carry that forward.

Living recklessly alive means honoring your worth, not because of what you've done but because of who you are. It's allowing yourself to take up space, to dream big dreams, to rest when you're tired, and to demand more from life simply because you deserve it. When you believe in your own value, you stop settling for less than what you need. You stop waiting for someone else to tell you that you're enough; instead, you say it to yourself and believe it.

So today, let your life reflect that truth. Say no when you need to. Ask for what you want. Let yourself be seen, even if your voice shakes. The goal isn't perfection; it's presence. It's waking up to the miracle that you're still here, still becoming, and already worthy of everything good and beautiful that life has to offer.

Let today be the day you stop shrinking, stop apologizing, and start owning your worth. The world doesn't need a perfect version of you; it needs the real one. Living recklessly alive begins with believing that who you are is already more than enough.

RECKLESSLY ALIVE AFFIRMATION

I AM ENOUGH, WITHOUT EXCEPTION. I HONOR MY WORTH BY SHOWING UP FULLY, JUST AS I AM.

REFLECTION

What will stick with you about owning your worth from this journey? How can you carry those lessons forward to create a life that feels vibrant and alive?

You can do this.

DAY 88

COME ALIVE THROUGH THE STRUGGLE

I THINK SOME OF THE MOST RESILIENT PEOPLE IN THE WORLD don't see themselves that way. To them, the struggle is normal, what they've always known. They'll shrug and say, "I didn't have a choice." But every day, they choose to rise again and push up from the ground one more time, carrying the weight of what tried to hold them down.

That kind of strength rarely looks heroic. It's the farmer tilling soil in the rain because the crops can't wait. It's the tired parent sitting at the kitchen table, helping their child with homework after a ten-hour shift. It's the person rebuilding after loss, piecing together something new from the wreckage. It's the simple act of continuing, even when life feels unrelenting.

Resilience doesn't always announce itself. Sometimes it looks like choosing to keep going when no one's watching. It's built in the moments when you decide to try again, even with shaky hands. It's there when you pause to rest, but don't quit. Without even realizing it, you've been gathering strength, one difficult moment at a time.

If you're struggling today, take a breath. And then take the smallest step to push yourself upward. You don't have to do it all at once, but don't doubt the power of this moment. Each time you rise, you remind the world and yourself that you are still here, moving forward with more resilience than you give yourself credit for.

That's the heartbeat of the recklessly alive life—to let the struggle shape you without letting it steal you. To hold the mess and the momentum at the same time. To refuse to let your story end in the hard part.

You've already done the impossible more times than you give yourself credit for. And if you're feeling tired or unsure today, let this truth land: Your resilience is real. It's in the laughter you found again, the boundaries you learned to set, the hope you still dare to hold.

RECKLESSLY ALIVE AFFIRMATION

MY STRENGTH IS IN HOW I RISE AFTER HARDSHIP.
I HONOR MY STORY AND THE RESILIENCE IT REFLECTS.

REFLECTION

What will stick with you about resilience from this journey? How can you carry those lessons forward to create a life that feels vibrant and alive?

You can do this.

DAY 89

ALIVE AND WORTHY OF CARE

SOMEWHERE ALONG THE WAY, WE WERE TAUGHT THAT SELF-CARE was something extra, like a reward for getting through the hard stuff or a luxury earned after burnout. But over the past few months, we've looked at self-care as something different—a form of protest against exhaustion.

Self-care is the decision to slow down when everything in you screams to keep performing. It's choosing to walk outside instead of spiraling. It's deciding to say, "I need help," or "I need a break," even when that feels uncomfortable.

Caring for yourself doesn't look the same for everyone, and it doesn't have to. For one person, it's journaling with coffee and morning light. For someone else, it's cleaning the house, moving their body, and texting the person who understands. Self-care shifts. It adapts. It asks, *What do I need today to keep feeling my best?*

Caring for yourself reflects a deep truth: You were never meant to just survive. You were meant to live fully. Your needs matter in the middle of the storm, not just once it's passed. Your health, your peace, your energy—are worth protecting now.

That voice inside you—the one that tells you to keep going, to try again, to believe—gets stronger and clearer when you tend to your own needs. When you stop running on fumes and start paying attention to what helps you feel whole, you can hear this truth a little louder: You can do this.

RECKLESSLY ALIVE AFFIRMATION

I CHOOSE TO HONOR MY NEEDS WITH COMPASSION AND CARE.

REFLECTION

What will stick with you about self-care from this journey? How can you carry those lessons forward to create a life that feels vibrant and alive?

You can do this.

THE PURPOSE IN FEELING FULLY ALIVE

THERE'S NO SINGULAR MOMENT WHEN PURPOSE DECLARES itself. No clean arrival point. No booming voice to confirm that you've finally made it. For most of us, purpose starts more like a persistent question. A pull. A shift in how you see the world and your place in it.

It's tempting to believe that it's something you have to chase down. Like one day you'll stumble into the right job, the right passion, the right set of circumstances, and everything will click. But purpose rarely works that way. It isn't a finish line; it's an unfolding that takes shape as you keep showing up for your life, even on the days when your life doesn't feel particularly meaningful.

You've already lived so many pieces of your purpose, in how you've helped someone, with no promise of reciprocation; in the boundaries you've learned to hold; and in the moments when you've chosen truth over comfort and kindness over approval. These things matter. Even if no one applauds them. Even if you're still figuring out what comes next.

There's a quiet kind of purpose found in the way you stay soft in a world that tells you to harden, or in how you create moments of joy and connection, without an audience, without needing it to be big. Purpose lives in how you move through the world when no one's watching.

Some days, purpose might feel like fire. Other days, it's a spark you're protecting from the wind. That's okay. Let it evolve. Let it catch you off guard. Let it stretch into the parts of your life you used to keep hidden.

You don't have to hold the whole plan. You don't need a title or tagline. All you need is the courage to take the next honest step, trusting that purpose isn't waiting at some finish line. It's already growing in the way you live, love, and choose to show up to this one wild life, recklessly alive.

RECKLESSLY ALIVE AFFIRMATION

I TRUST THAT MY PURPOSE UNFOLDS WITH EVERY STEP I TAKE.

REFLECTION

What will stick with you about purpose from this journey? How can you carry those lessons forward to create a life that feels vibrant and alive?

You can do this.

DEEP AND MEANINGFUL CONNECTIONS

SOME OF THE MOST MEANINGFUL MOMENTS IN LIFE BEGIN WITH A simple act: reaching toward someone else. Not with guarantees or with a script but just with the hope that something honest might take root between you.

Connection is what gives life its depth and meaning: the laughter shared across a dinner table, the steady presence of someone who shows up when you need them most, the vulnerable conversations, which remind us that we're not alone. Living recklessly alive means leaning in to these moments, even when it feels risky or requires you to go first.

True connection isn't always easy. It asks for honesty and courage. It asks you to open up and share pieces of yourself, even when you're unsure of how they'll be received. But the beauty of connection lies in its imperfection. Showing up doesn't require perfect words or a polished version of yourself. What matters is the willingness to be real, with your flaws, your fears, your full humanity, and to offer others the same space.

Think about the connections that have shaped you. They weren't built in a single moment but over time, in the small acts of care and kindness, in the moments when someone made you feel seen. These relationships remind us that life is better when shared and that our stories are richer when intertwined with others' stories.

As you move forward, choose to prioritize connection. Be the one who reaches out, offers kindness, and dares to go deeper. Not every moment will lead to something lasting, but each one will remind you of the beauty of being human. Living recklessly alive is rooted in creating those moments on purpose, because in the end, it's the love we give and the people we share it with that matter most.

RECKLESSLY ALIVE AFFIRMATION

I CHOOSE TO LIVE OPEN TO OTHERS, BELIEVING THAT REAL CONNECTION IS WORTH THE RISK.

REFLECTION

What will stick with you about connection from this journey? How can you carry those lessons forward to create a life that feels vibrant and alive?

You can do this.

THE BEGINNING OF WHAT'S NEXT

YOU MADE A DECISION TO BEGIN. NOT BECAUSE YOU HAD IT ALL figured out but because something inside you whispered that it was time. Time to move, grow, and reach for a life that feels more like your own. And now here you are, standing at the edge of this journey, looking back at how far you've come.

You've taken bold action, not just in the big leaps but in the choice to keep going. You've rewritten the words you speak to yourself. You've let go of the ones that never belonged. You've come home to your worth without needing to earn it.

You've learned to call your strength by its name. The kind of resilience that doesn't need to be flashy to be real. You've started tending to your life instead of outrunning it, caring for your mind, your body, and your spirit, even in small ways—especially in small ways.

You've reimagined purpose, not as something to chase but as something you live. And maybe most of all, you've let yourself reach toward connection. You've taken the risk to be seen, to be known, to belong again.

Maybe some days felt like you were climbing a mountain in the fog, unsure if the summit was even there. But that's one of life's greatest wonders: You don't have to see the whole path to take the next step.

This journey has always been a steady return to what matters. And now, whatever comes next, you're not starting from scratch. You're moving forward with more tools, more truth, more of yourself intact.

This isn't the end. It's the beginning of what's next. And when the road feels steep again, and it will, you'll know how to breathe through it. You'll remember who you are. And you'll be able to say to yourself, with everything in you:

You can do this.

ACKNOWLEDGMENTS

TO KARA, MY ACQUISITIONS EDITOR: THANK YOU FOR YOUR GUIDance and for helping cast the vision for this book before others could see it. Your belief in this message made all the difference.

To Cheryl: Thank you for seeing something in my writing and advocating to get my voice in front of the people who need it most. Your support opened doors I didn't know how to knock on.

To Jenn: Your editing made this book stronger in every way. Thank you for your clarity, care, and thoughtful attention to every detail.

To my family and chosen family: Thank you for standing with me through the hard days, for holding space, and for reminding me who I am when I forget. Your love is stitched into every chapter.

To the incredible team at HarperCollins: Thank you for your partnership, creativity, and care in bringing this project to life. I'm deeply grateful to be on this journey with you.

To everyone fighting to spread awareness about mental health and suicide prevention: Your work saves lives. Thank you for your courage, your voice, and your relentless hope.

To all the heroes who've walked with me on my healing journey: Thank you for helping me process my trauma, reclaim my voice, and turn pain into purpose. You've made it possible for me to help others choose to stay.

And to every reader who has dared to believe that something more is possible: You're why I wrote this. Keep going.

ABOUT THE AUTHOR

SAM EATON IS AN AUTHOR, A SPEAKER, AND THE FOUNDER OF THE Recklessly Alive Foundation, a suicide prevention organization sprinting toward a world with zero deaths by suicide. He has spoken at more than 250 events across the United States, sharing his story of overcoming depression and offering hope to others walking similar paths. Sam holds a master's degree in educational leadership and leads the foundation's work to equip communities to have real conversations about mental health.

He is the author of *Recklessly Alive* (2020) and *Healing Out Loud* (2025), books that blend personal storytelling with practical encouragement for anyone navigating the messy, beautiful work of living life to the fullest. Sam lives in Minneapolis, Minnesota, where he enjoys collecting vinyl records, lifting moderately heavy weights, and trying every flavor of Oreo.

To learn more about Sam's work,
visit recklesslyalive.com or follow
@recklesslyalive on Instagram and TikTok.